The Etiquette of Engagement and Marriage

Describing Modern Manners and Customs of Courtship and Marriage, and giving Full Details regarding the Wedding Ceremony and Arra

G. R. M. DevereuxYour text here 3

CHAPTER I

The Beginnings of Courtship--Favourable Opportunities--Intellectual Affinity--Artistic Fellowship--Athletic Comradeship--Amateur Acting--Social Intercourse--Different Ideas of Etiquette.

Who can fix the exact time at which Courtship begins? It may or may not be preceded by Love; it may coincide with the birth of the tender passion; it may possibly be well in advance of Cupid's darts; or, sad to say, it may be little more than the prelude to a purely business transaction.

Opportunities.

Men and women meet each other on very varied planes, and each walk in life has its own opportunities. The intellectually minded may begin their courtship over musty books or choice editions, and advanced students will make love as ardently as a country maid and her rustic lover. A dry mathematical problem may be as good a medium for the lover as a nosegay or a verse of poetry.

A Love of the Arts

implies an emotional element that lends itself to love-making. Music is responsible for a great deal. The passion of the love-song, the pathos of the composer so easily become the language of the interpreter, when love is in the heart.

Athletic Comradeship.

The fascinations of Art are more sensuous than the vigorous, breezy pleasures of outdoor pursuits. For healthy-minded love-making this comradeship yields golden opportunities. {17} The outdoor pair may not look so sentimental as the artistic couple; but their hearts may be as tender and their love as true, though their hands meet over the mending of a tyre or the finding of a tennis ball instead of being clasped in the ecstasy born of sweet sounds.

Amateur Acting.

I know of an Amateur Dramatic Society that has been nicknamed the Matrimonial Club from the number of marriages that have taken place among the members. This amusement does pave the way for courtship, for in no other are the conventionalities so completely set aside for the time being. Those who have thus been brought together in make-believe are not always anxious to resume formal relations. Acting affords priceless opportunities.

Making up his Mind.

Now when a man has made up his mind that he wants to marry a certain girl, he emerges from the indefinite stage of observation, admiration, or flirtation, and begins to make his intentions known. In view of the impossibility of a universal law of etiquette, it may be said that the remarks in these pages apply to that largest section of society known as the middle classes.

When a man is in a position to marry, he should be especially careful not to single out a girl by his attentions if he does not intend to propose to her, for the way in which his conduct is regarded will be greatly influenced by his banking account, and one with a small income and smaller prospects may do things with impunity that a man in more affluent circumstances could not do without the risk of having a serious construction put upon them.

"Ineligibles."

I once heard a very rich young man bewail his fate on this score. He said: "A fellow with only a hundred a year gets all the fun. He can talk to any nice girl he likes as much as he likes, and nothing is said, because people know he can't marry. But if you have a little money (*his* ran into thousands) {18} they say you're engaged the second time you're seen with a lady!"

This may sound mercenary, but after all it is only practical. When it is known that a man neither is nor is likely to be in a position to marry, parents encourage his visits to the house, or permit his attentions to their daughters, at their own risk. Not that lack of means will prevent falling in love--far from it! When parents think marriage impossible they sometimes give opportunities to an *ineligible*, and then are aggrieved at his making good use of them.

There are many things to be considered at the beginning of courtship. Much must depend upon the family of the lady.

Social Intercourse.

In a household where there is neither father nor brother on the scene a man must walk warily. He is sure to be chaffed about any special intimacy with such a family, and even well-meant chaff sometimes spoils a situation. A woman who has no grown-up son, and has lost, or is temporarily separated from, her husband, will do well to avoid any undue eagerness in cultivating masculine society. She should exercise her own intuition, and extend a cordial, unaffected welcome to such men as she thinks suitable friends, or possible husbands, for her daughters. She should be equally careful to eschew any sign of match-making intrigue or narrow-minded suspicion. If she is the right sort of mother the men will probably find in her a charming companion and valuable friend.

It is most essential that girls who have been mainly brought up under feminine influences should have ample and varied opportunities of learning something about the other sex, by personal intercourse, before there is any question of their marriage. If this is not done it will be found that they generally fall a prey to the first suitor who comes along. They have formed unreal, impossible, and often foolish ideas about men, and are unable to distinguish the tares from the wheat. A girl with brothers or men friends is far more likely to make a wise choice than one who has formed her ideas from heroes of fiction.

Where a man is introduced by the son of the house, his path is on smoother ground. As "Charlie's chum" he has a {19} perfectly reasonable and innocent excuse for his frequent visits, even though Charlie may receive a minimum of his attention. On the other hand, fathers and brothers are not always aids to courtship. They hold different views about the man to those of their womenkind, and *may* make things unpleasant for all parties. A man can soon establish himself as a sort of oracle in a feminine circle, and has countless chances of making himself useful to the ladies. He may have to consider the proprieties a little more, but then he is master of the situation, with none of his own kind to point out the weak joints in his armour.

Tact.

A tactful suitor will be courteous to every member of his sweetheart's family. He will not for a moment let it be thought that he considers her the only one worthy of his notice. Even younger brothers and sisters are preferable as allies, and it will make the whole position much pleasanter if he is liked by her own people. He will especially make it his business to stand well with her parents. By prettily filial attentions to Mollie's mother his cause will be materially strengthened, and though the young lady may grudge the time he spends in discussing politics or stocks and shares with her father, her own common sense will tell her that it is a very good investment for the future. Moreover, a really nice-minded girl would never tolerate a man who was discourteous to her parents, however flattering his attitude might be to herself.

A Breach of Etiquette.

When a girl is staying with friends, no man should pay his addresses to her unknown to her hostess or against that lady's wishes. It is better to end a visit than to abuse hospitality. The hostess is responsible to her visitor's parents for the time being, and the lovers should consider her position. Whatever social or domestic restrictions may stand between a man and the woman he wishes to woo, he must pay a certain regard to them for her sake, if not for his own. No two households are regulated by the same code in the smaller details of etiquette.

{20} In one family old-world notions of decorum prevail, and the lover will want self-restraint and prudence; in another the law of liberty reigns supreme, and the young people do pretty much as they like. In such a circle the lover's presence will be taken for granted--one more or less does not matter--and courtship is made easy. Man being by nature a hunter who values his spoils in proportion to the dangers and difficulties overcome in the chase, is not always so keen to secure the quarry that costs the least effort, so the free and easy parents often find that their daughters remain unmarried.

CHAPTER II

Introductions--Recognition of Affinity, or Love at First Sight--How to Follow up an Acquaintance--Kindly Offices of Relations and Friends.

Introductions.

There are definite laws of etiquette in the matter of introductions. A man has seen the lady once, or, it may be, has watched her from a distance with longing eyes for months past. He may not make himself known to her without the aid of a third person, who should first ascertain whether his acquaintance will be agreeable to the object of his admiration. It may happen that the gods will send him some lucky chance of rendering her a timely service. He might rescue her dog from a canine street fray, pick up a trinket she had dropped, or, better still, like the people in novels, travel with her on a long journey and prove himself a tactful cavalier. Under any of these circumstances the ice would be broken, and possibly an informal introduction would take place. It ought, however, to be supplemented by more regular proceedings before any recognised intercourse is possible.

A girl is not supposed to ask for an introduction to a man, but--low be it spoken--she often does; not publicly, of course, but she simply confides in her married lady friend or favourite brother, neither of whom would naturally give her away.

A man ought not to haunt a girl whose acquaintance he wishes to make. There is a wide margin between accepting invitations to houses, or turning up opportunely at parties where he may expect to meet her, and walking obtrusively past her house several times a day, or shadowing her out shopping and at public places of amusement. A very young girl {22} might think this romantic, though youth is terribly matter-of-fact nowadays. Her elders would certainly consider it rude, and put him down as a man to be avoided. An elderly sentimental spinster would be in a flutter. A level-headed girl would think him a bore, if not a bit of a fool.

Love at First Sight.

This seems a very large order, for love means so much. That there is often a wondrous *recognition of affinity*, a sort of flash from soul to soul kindling the desire for closer union, is undeniable. A man suddenly sees the one whom he resolves to win for his wife. A woman realises that she has found the man of all others to whom she would gladly give herself. This is not love; it is but the herald that goes before the king.

Opinions on the subject of marrying one's first love are much divided, and one has rather to beg the question by saying that it is mainly a matter of temperament. The age at which you begin falling in love has also to be taken into account. A modern writer gives it as his opinion that "A wise man will never marry his first love, for he knows that matrimony demands as much special attention as any of the learned professions. Unqualified amateurs swell the lists of the divorce court."

The Man's Case.

It may be taken for granted that the man who has some experience of women and their ways makes a better lover than one who knows nothing of them. Love may supply him with essentials, but only practice can perfect details. A man of five-and-twenty may be supposed to know his own mind.

The Girl's Case.

The girl in her teens who gives her love and herself may find full satisfaction in her marriage; but blind self-confidence and impulsive inexperience may lay up a store of sorrow for the future. No man is wise to hurry a young girl into marriage.

{23}

How to follow up an Acquaintance.

Once the introduction is over it remains mainly with the man to make the most of his advantages. He obtains permission to call; and it is not a bad plan to allow a short interval to elapse before availing himself of the privilege. He must not seem neglectful, but may wait just long enough to give the lady time to think about him, to wonder, to wish, to long for his coming. He will be careful not to transgress any detail of etiquette in this his first call, but he will not leave without having made some distinct advance, having found some pretext for a less formal visit. He will convey to her in a subtle, meaning manner that the sun will not shine for him till he sees her again.

Her Family.

He will find out what interests her people. He will bring her father rare cuttings for his garden, or introduce him to a choice brand of cigars. He will lend her mother books, sing or recite at her pet charity entertainments, or even make a martyr of himself at flower-shows and bazaars. He will bring designs for her sister's wood-carving, or teach small Tommy to ride a bicycle.

As to the lady of his heart, he will begin by sharing her pursuits only as a means to an end, for when love-making once steps in other pursuits are neglected, if not totally shelved, for the time being. This transition stage requires great tact. He must not startle her by too sudden a development. Some women may like to be taken by storm, to be married by capture as it were, but the average girl likes to have time to enjoy being wooed and won. She basks in the gradual unfolding of his love; she rejoices over each new phase of their courtship; she lingers longingly on the threshold of her great happiness. She is intoxicated by the sense of her own power; she is touched by the deference which curbs his ardour.

Kindly Offices of Relations and Friends.

Outsiders can often make or mar a possible marriage. When the third person undertakes to introduce two people in a case {24} where even a one-sided attraction is supposed to exist, no remark should be made about it. The lady friend who tells a girl that a man "is very much taken with her," strikes a fatal blow at the unconscious grace with which the girl would otherwise have received him. The blundering brother who blurts out: "My sister says that girl's awfully gone on you, old chap!" probably makes his chum fight shy of the girl, or indulge in a little fun at her expense. It should be remembered that a nearer acquaintance does not always confirm impressions formed at a distance.

A sister who will discreetly play the part of Number Three is invaluable. A brother who will bring the man home to dinner, or arrange cycling expeditions, is a treasure. The aunt who gives dances or river parties just when he has his holiday is inestimable. The uncle who has a fancy for stage managing, and casts the two for the lovers' parts in a charmingly unconscious fashion, is a relation worth having. Married friends on either side can afford many extra and delightful opportunities of meeting. While thus smoothing the path of love, all obtrusive allusion to the suspected or recognised state of things should be carefully avoided. It is an unpardonable breach of etiquette for any one to draw attention to the movements of a couple by a laugh, a nod, or a wink which, though not intended to reach them, gives frequent rise to unpleasant situations. Her friends should guard against anything savouring of a husband-trap; his friends should avoid any indication that they look upon her as his lawful prey.

There should be no questionable chaff or talking at the possible lovers. Older people who have forgotten how tender their own sensibilities once were are rather fond of cracking jokes, and make tactless, pointed remarks. The old friend of the family who slaps the prospective suitor on the back, and in the lady's presence challenges him to kiss her under the mistletoe, only succeeds in making them both uncomfortable. The elderly relative who nods her cap, saying: "Oh yes, we know all about it! We were young ourselves once!" probably has the best intentions, but has chosen the worst way of showing them.

CHAPTER III

Intercourse between Unconfessed Lovers--The Question of Presents--Exchange of Hospitality--The Man who lives at Home--The Man in Rooms.

Unconfessed Lovers.

There is a fascinating, yet withal tormenting, insecurity in the intercourse preceding an actual Declaration of Love. It may be the ante-chamber to an earthly paradise. It may but prove to be a fool's paradise. George Eliot describes two of her characters as being "in that stage of courtship which makes the most exquisite moment of youth, the freshest blossom-time of passion--when each is sure of the other's love and all its mutual divination, exalting the most trivial word, the slightest gesture into thrills delicate and delicious as wafted jasmine scent."

It may be that he has some honourable reason to forbid his speaking when he would. He may fear to lose her altogether if he is too hasty. Possibly there is another man in the case. She may be revelling in the new joy of life without analysing its source. If she has faced the secret of her own heart she will mount guard over herself lest word or look should betray her, before he has told her that she does not love in vain.

Breaches of Etiquette.

When a man finds that his attentions are unwelcome, and a woman has used every means in her power, short of actual rudeness, to show him that she does not desire his nearer acquaintance, he has no right to force himself or his love upon her. He has no right to make sure of any woman's love before he has asked her for it, unless, of course, she has {26} betrayed herself by an unwomanly want of reticence. It is both foolish and ill-bred for him to play the part of dog-in-the-manger and to object to her receiving attentions from any one else. Until he has declared himself he can assume no control over the disposal of her favours, still less should he stoop to put a spoke in another man's wheel.

The Question of Presents.

A line must be carefully drawn between the gifts of an unconfessed lover and of a *fiancé*. The former may send flowers, bon-bons, and pretty trifles of that sort, or he could give her a dog or a Persian kitten; but he must not offer her articles of jewellery or any item of her toilette. He might give her the undressed skin of an animal that he had shot, but he could not order a set of furs to be sent to her from a shop. It must be remembered that ostensibly they are as yet only friends, and though every gift will have its inward meaning, it should not have any outward significance.

In offering a present the unconfessed lover will do well to enclose a little note [footnote in original: For those who wish to study the art of letter-writing there is a most excellent guide to all sorts of correspondence, entitled, "How Shall I Word It?" published at one shilling by C. Arthur Pearson (Limited).] couched in some such terms as these:

"Dear Miss Grayson,--You said the other day that you could not grow lilies of the valley in your garden, so I am venturing to send you the accompanying basket, which I hope you will be kind enough to accept.--Believe me, sincerely yours,   Duncan Talbot."

Exchange of Hospitality.

Where both families are acquainted, and in a similar social position, the interchange of hospitality will probably be somewhat increased in virtue of the growing intimacy between the possible lovers. Until there is an acknowledged engagement it would not be etiquette for his family to single her out from the rest of her own people by inviting her alone. A parent,

{27} brother, or sister ought to be included. It would also be diplomatic on the part of her friends not to extend too gushing a welcome to him, while they take his belongings as a matter of course. Because the one family can give dinner parties it does not follow that the other should not afford just as much enjoyment by a simpler form of hospitality. The possible lover does not come to criticise the cuisine of the household in which the object of his desires is to be seen.

The Man Who Lives at Home.

It will often happen that a man makes acquaintances who become friends quite independently of his own family. But if he is seriously contemplating matrimony he will be anxious to introduce his chosen one to his womenkind. Supposing that his people were the older residents in the place, he would pave the way by saying that his mother, or sister, as the case might be, would so much like to call, and might she do so? Unless there should be some purely feminine feud the permission would be cordially given. If, on the other hand, the girl's family were the first comers to the locality he would then ask the lady to call on his people, intimating that they were longing to know her and her daughter, and what a personal gratification it would be to him to bring the desired meeting about. In the present day the old hard and fast rules which used to regulate calling are no longer observed. If acquaintance is really sought there will be no difficulty for a woman of tact and judgment to cultivate it.

A Danger.

Women are very quick to see when they are being courted for their sons or brothers, and they do not always like it. It is discourteous, and very transparent, to send an invitation to a girl the day after her brother has come home on leave in which you hope "that Captain Boyle will be able to accompany her," when practically you have ignored her existence since the last time he was at home. It is not kind or considerate to try and monopolise the society of any man whose {28} business or profession only permits of his being at home at long intervals. A girl may want to have him with her very much indeed, but she should not be piqued and feel injured if he excuses himself on the ground of having to take his sister out, or spend his evening with his parents. He will be all the better husband for this courtesy to his own relations. Of course his people may be very dull, possibly unpleasant, and in that case real friendship will be a labour, if not an impossibility; but, for the man's sake, they must be treated in such a way as not to hurt either his feelings or their own. The same, naturally, holds good with regard to her belongings.

The Man who Lives in Rooms

is a much easier person to cultivate. You take it for granted that he is dull, that his dinners are not well cooked, and that he misses the delights of home. So you ask him to drop in when he likes. "We are nearly always in to tea;" or "We dine at 7.30, and if you take us as we are, there will be a place for you." As soon as a man sees that this sort of invitation is really meant he will not be slow to avail himself of it. Not that he will come to dinner every other night, but he will drop in to tea, and turn up in the course of the evening for a little music and a chat. He gets into the habit of coming in on Sunday afternoons, and generally ends by staying to supper.

As a Host.

All this means a great deal to a lone bachelor, and makes him long for a home of his own. In return for this delightful hospitality he will, perhaps, ask a sister to stay with him and give a tea-party in his rooms. Later on he will have seats for a theatre, and arrange a nice little dinner or supper in town. Where dramatic delights are out of reach he will plan a river or cycling expedition, he will entertain his friends at a local cricket match, he will inspire his fellow bachelors to give a dance; and there will be only one guest whose presence is of any importance to him.

He will not let it appear that he is paying a debt; he will {29} imply, rather, that the ladies are conferring a favour upon him. He will consult her mother as to many arrangements, and make sure that all the guests are to her liking. He will not be afraid of asking a possible rival, who might be more dangerous when absent than present. While thus entertaining the lady of his choice, the suitor must discern nicely between paying her special honour and taking it for granted that she already belongs to him. He must not advertise the fact that the party is given for her, by neglecting his other guests, or by omitting pleasant courtesies to less-favoured maidens.

CHAPTER IV

Intercourse with (1) The Home Girl; (2) The Bachelor Girl; (3) The Business Girl; (4) The Student or Professional Girl--Friends who become Lovers.

The Home Girl.

As has already been said, the would-be lover will do well to study the workings of his lady's home. If she has many domestic duties to perform he will arrange his spare time to fit in with hers. He will not call at such times as would be inconvenient and run the risk of ructions, simply because he knows *she* will be glad to see him. He will not look aggrieved if she refuses to go out cycling with him because she has promised to take the little ones out blackberrying. He will seize a golden chance and go with them. When he is at her home, he will not act as if the whole place belonged to him, and he will be careful not to become a bore.

Men of leisure, and men whose professions place them on confidential terms, such as doctors and clergymen, have the greatest opportunities of knowing the Home Girl at her best, and at her worst. The last two see her under conditions that show what she is really made of, and not merely what she appears in society, for they have access to the house in times of trouble when outsiders are excluded.

The Bachelor Girl

is pretty sure to be out of her teens, but not necessarily in the thirties. She will probably have girl chums who, like herself, are living in a more or less independent fashion. She sometimes indulges in anti-matrimonial theories, and it may prove most interesting to convert her from the error of her ways. A man has such beautifully sure ground under his feet when she has given him plainly to understand that she prefers {31} friendship to love. A would-be suitor will find his opportunities of intercourse regulated by her standard of conventionality. She is free to make her own life, with her own code of conduct, her own ideas of responsibility.

She meets him frankly on what she deems common ground; but he sees the other side of things, for men and women never can and never will look at life from the same point of view. His knowledge should make him all the more jealous of her fair fame, but he must walk warily lest he wound her womanly dignity. She will do nothing wrong, her heart is too pure for that, but he must not let her do what may even appear to be wrong. At first she will be a little intoxicated with the sense of her own freedom. He must never take advantage of that, for he knows that the woman always pays.

They will probably include one of her chums in their cosy tea-parties at her rooms, and there will be no secret of his coming and going. He will see her home from the theatre, concert, or lecture, but he will not go and smoke in her flat till the small hours. He will discriminate as to the restaurant where they have lunch together, and he will not invite her to a *tête-à-tête* supper after the play. She will entertain him at her club, and he will guard against the assumption of rights that are not his.

The Business Girl.

The daily life of the Business Girl is of necessity a regular one, and the man who wants to know more of her knows where to find her. If by chance he is employed in the same firm, he has daily chances of making headway with her. He can often render her little services, help her over rough places, and make life as pleasant again for her. All this can be so managed that no one, save perhaps a lynx-eyed rival, will know anything about it. He will certainly not make her the talk of the office by bragging of his conquest, and laying wagers as to his chance of success, or get her into hot water by hindering her at her work.

She will keep her own counsel, and not giggle with other girls when he comes along. Of course she will tell her special friend all about it, for what is the good of a love-affair if you cannot talk to some one on the all-engrossing subject?

{32} She will not display the buttonhole he bought her on the way from the train to all the other girls as his gift, nor will she be foolish and give herself away by hanging about his room door in the hopes of seeing him. She will always find time for a word or a bright glance when they do meet, by accident of course.

He will not make her conspicuous by always travelling home with her, but he will be at hand to pilot her through a fog, to help her out of a crowd, or to get her a place when there is anything to be seen. He will make it plain that he thinks of her, and is ever on the alert to play the part of her cavalier.

She is practical and self-reliant, as a rule, but she does not object to be courted. When they plan a Saturday outing she will not propose what she knows to be beyond his means, but she will pardon him for a little extravagance in her honour.

Social Inequality.

When a man in a superior position begins paying attentions to a girl filling a subordinate post, he will probably expose her to the jealousy, and possible malice, of her fellows; but this will depend greatly upon the girl herself. In this case the suitor must steer clear of anything like patronage. If she is worthy of his notice she is worthy of his respect and consideration. He will be careful not to take her to any place of amusement where she would feel out of her element, or run the risk of being snubbed by any of his own rich friends. The son of a wealthy merchant would not give as much pleasure to a girl earning thirty shillings in his father's office if he took her to supper at the Carlton, as if he selected some less magnificent restaurant. She would feel more at home on the river, or at Earl's Court, than on the lawn at Hurlingham. He would show her that his pleasure was to be with her, and he would wait till he could call her his wife before introducing her to a new world.

The Student or Professional Girl.

There is a little country called Bohemia, whose laws rule the kingdom of Art, and whose government seems a trifle erratic to those who live outside the charmed circle. Students of {33} music, painting, sculpture, and the drama have a code of Etiquette that may be called adaptable; but it does not follow that because a man is an artist he must therefore be deficient in courtesy to women; nor is it yet inevitable that when a girl develops a talent for drawing she should violate all the proprieties.

Falling in love with music-masters is a very old story, but it is not quite a thing of the past. A man has no right to work on the emotions of his pupil merely for his own amusement or to gratify his vanity. He may find that it infuses more soul into her music, but she is a woman as well as an artist. Where both have the artistic temperament highly developed, it is playing with fire indeed.

The Dramatic Student is thrown into very mixed society. She is left with a great deal of spare time on her hands when merely understudying, or out of an engagement. She is forced to keep late hours, and may be exposed to many unpleasant experiences. I know of one man who was so distressed at the girl of his heart having to cross London by the last 'bus every night that he changed his quarters and took rooms as near to where she was living as he could, in order to be able to see her home without making the fact unduly conspicuous.

This was a delicate act of courtesy, and I am glad to say that they are now happily married.

The Medical Student and Hospital Nurse are generally women with a special turn of mind, and in the former case the work of training is so absorbing that it can hardly be run concurrently with the delights of courtship. The nurse soon learns to take care of herself, and has many special opportunities of studying the lords of creation. She sees some of the noblest and most gifted of them at their work, the wildest of them at play, and all and sundry in their hour of weakness; and this experience should be borne in mind by the man who seeks to win her. She will not regard him as a demi-god, nor as a hero of romance. She will not appeal to the man who wants a mere plaything in his wife. She will have far higher gifts than the society doll, but she will be a woman to be wooed, and worth the winning.

{34}

Friends who become Lovers.

There are those who say that friendship excludes love, and there is a kind of friendship which can only exist where love is impossible and undesired. On the other hand we know that sometimes the boy and girl who have grown up side by side, who have shared each other's pranks and penalties, do wake up one day to find a new element asserting itself in their intercourse. A certain shyness springs up between them only to be dispelled by fuller, sweeter comradeship. This development sometimes takes place during a period of separation, or when a possible rival appears on the scene. It usually assumes concrete form in the man's mind first. He may hide his love under the guise of friendship till he feels he has a right to make it known. It may be that he has to go abroad to seek the wherewithal to start a home, and when he has succeeded he will write some such letter as this:--

"My Dear Clari,--When I threw up my berth at home you wondered why I was in such a hurry to leave the old country, and home, and you, and it was very hard not to tell you the real reason. I came out here to make enough money to set up housekeeping, and, dear, I want you to come and help me, now I have succeeded so far. I know it is a tremendous thing to ask, and that I am entirely unworthy of the sacrifice you would be making; but, dear, we know each other pretty well by this, and I hope you can trust yourself to me. If you only knew how I have longed to tell you this through the last two years of our sweet, but to me unsatisfying, friendship you would not keep me in suspense any longer than you can help. You have been the one thought and object of my life ever since I came out, and I have lived in fear of some other fellow getting in before me.

I think I must always have loved you, it seems a part of myself, but it was your first ball that woke me up.

Let me know soon, dear.--Ever and always your devoted

"GORDON."

However the change from friendship to love comes about, the man must be just as courteous as if she had only crossed {35} his path in the fulness of her young womanhood. He must not take her for granted because he knew her in pinafores, nor slight her sensibilities because he taught her to climb trees. If he is negligent other men will supply his deficiencies. As a lover he is bound to appear in a new light, and he must look to it that he does not suffer by the change. The friend ought to make the best lover, for he knows the tastes and weaknesses, the temperament and surroundings of the woman he has chosen. They will be bound by countless old associations, but this very familiarity may breed, not contempt, but a matter-of-fact mental attitude that will rob courtship of more than half its charm.

CHAPTER V

Flirts, Male and Female--He Changes his Mind on the Verge of a Proposal--How She accepts the Situation--How She may give Encouragement or ward off an Unwelcome Offer.

It may be questioned whether there is any etiquette in flirtation. Yes, I think there is. Flirts of both sexes may be divided into two large classes--(1) the wanton and deliberate; (2) the kindly and spontaneous.

Flirts.

The first class are birds of prey. The man is probably very charming, a delightful companion, an ideal cavalier, a man whose society a woman always enjoys--especially if she does not take him seriously. It is she who fails to realise that she is only one of a large number who fall victims and suffer accordingly. She blissfully accepts his subtle suggestion that she is *the* one woman in the world for him--so she is while they are together--and flatters herself that though he may have flirted with others he is really in love with her. When once the sport of the moment is over he leaves his prey, more or less cruelly wounded, and gaily seeks new fields for his prowess. This sort of man likes young and inexperienced girls or women whose confiding trust exceeds their power of discernment.

It is an unpardonable breach of etiquette for a man to abuse hospitality and the privilege of intercourse by wanton conduct of this kind.

Making a Girl Conspicuous.

A man should remember that it is the woman who suffers from the breath of slander or the pettiness of gossip. Such {37} things affect him but little, if at all. Suppose that two young people belong to a public tennis or dramatic club. The man singles out one particular girl by his attentions, makes a point of always seeing her home, establishes himself as her constant cavalier, and thus puts it in the power of the gossips to say "Well, if they are not engaged they ought to be!" After a time he cools off, for no other reason than that he is tired of the girl or has possibly seen a fresh and more attractive face. It may have dawned upon him that he might be asked his intentions, and he does not care to confess that he never had any. This course of action is especially unfair in the case of a young girl whose experience of men's ways is but beginning. An older woman ought to be able to take care of herself, and if she thinks such a game worth the candle, no one can blame the man for helping her to play it.

The Female Flirt.

A woman in the first class of flirts is possibly more dangerous than the man. She has no heart, only insatiable vanity. She uses her powers on all who come in her way, regardless of any claim another of her sex may have upon them. Lover, husband, and friend, they are all fair game for her, and if hearts are damaged, well, she is always sure that her own will remain intact. Her veracity is as elastic as her conscience. Her charms are equalled by her unscrupulousness.

She will keep the youth in bondage without the slightest intention of ever marrying him. She will fool the mature man who is desperately in earnest, while she is angling after some one wealthier or more amusing. If she does elect to wed one of her victims, it is, in all probability, only to carry out her devastating tactics on a larger scale.

Kindly, Spontaneous Flirts.

The members of the second class, men and women, are charming without being dangerous. They love the society of the other sex; they have the art of pleasing and make use of it, but they play the game fairly. There is no poaching, no snares are laid for the unwary, and if harm is done it is because people have misunderstood them. The man flirts because he loves {38} to say pretty things to a woman. He revels in an interchange of banter and repartee which makes her eyes sparkle and his pulses beat the faster. The girl flirts out of the abundance of her joyous vitality. She suits herself to the companion of the hour. She knows nothing of the tender passion, she is not taking life quite seriously yet, but she has the delicacy to draw back when she sees danger signals in the eyes or the lingering clasp of her friend's hand. She will not make a fool of him. She is too straight for that.

Withdrawing Gracefully.

It is no easy matter to change the course of things when one has drifted into a flirtation. It behoves a girl then to choose her man carefully, and not to place herself in any false position towards him. If he is not chivalrous enough to take a delicately conveyed hint, he will only imagine that she is playing a more subtle game of coquetry, and by redoubling his attentions make himself the reverse of agreeable. No man with any regard for the most elementary rules of etiquette would either embarrass a lady by keeping up a tone that she had even indirectly discouraged, or insult her by insinuating that she had led him on.

He Changes his Mind on the Verge of a Proposal.

This is bound to be an awkward development for both parties, and it will take all a man's tact to avoid giving pain, and possibly gaining credit for having behaved badly. It is, nevertheless, the best time for a change to come. It may be that he has idealised the object of his attentions, looked at her through eyes blinded by her beauty, or dazzled by her fascination. He has not stopped to think what sort of woman she really is, what lies beneath that fair exterior. Then the word is spoken, the action witnessed, the mood revealed which makes him shrink from the thought of making her his wife.

His Way of Escape.

He will either seek safety in flight after a perfectly polite, but clearly-defined farewell; or he will gradually withdraw {39} from the terms of intimacy upon which he has stood. In no way must he be discourteous either to the lady or her friends.

Slow Awakening.

A man may change his mind almost imperceptibly. He will not turn against the woman, but he will realise that she can never be more to him than a friend, a genial chum. The cause of this is most likely the advent of the right woman. Force of contrast has a way of sorting people out. He will tell his friend the truth, and she will like him all the better for his confidence in her.

How She Accepts the Situation.

A brave, self-respecting woman will not like being left any more than her weaker sister, but she will take the blow standing, and be able to rejoice in the happiness of others. She will face her own sorrow alone and will utter no sound of complaint. It is an impertinence for acquaintances to condole with her. The sympathy of her loved ones will be hard enough to bear. She will be perfectly loyal to the woman her friend has chosen.

How She may give Encouragement.

There are women who leave the men very little to do in the way of courtship. Encouragement can, however, he given in a true womanly fashion. She can wear his flowers in preference to any others, and may judiciously let him see that she has kept the best in water after the dance. She will accept his escort and receive his attentions graciously, so as to show that they are valued.

Due Reserve.

She should never bestow effusive attentions on her lover, nor boast of his devotion to her. She may let him see that he stands well with her without telling him that he comes first. It is good for him to see that other men are in the running, and she must not let her feeling for him lead her into {40} discourtesy to any one else. She can let him do the wooing without being either haughty or capricious, for no man likes a woman who openly runs after him.

Transparent Devices.

A nice-minded girl does not always try to detach her lover from the rest of the company, though she enjoys a *tête-à-tête* as much as he does. She does not want to be sent with him on fictitious errands to the bottom of the garden. She leaves him to find the opportunities, and has a horror of her matchmaking relations.

How She may Ward off an Unwelcome Offer.

It is commonly agreed that a woman ought to be able to do this in the vast majority of cases. Her own intuition is seldom at fault. Even at the eleventh hour she may save the situation by a timely jest, a kindly bit of inconsequence, a sudden humorous inspiration--not at his expense, of course--and the man who is not a fool will see that it is not the psychological moment. Above all she must avoid being alone with him. Let her keep a child at her side, pay attention to the greatest bore, listen with grateful patience to the most prosy person she knows, rather than leave the ground clear for him. She should not go for moonlight strolls, nor to look for the Southern Cross on board ship, if she really wants to stave off his proposal. There is no need to be rude, and even if she has to appear unsympathetic, that is better than to humiliate him by a rejection. Some women glory over their hapless suitors as an Indian counts his scalps. This is the height of bad taste and heartlessness. We may be forgiven for hoping that they get left in the end themselves.

CHAPTER VI

The Question of Age--Young Lovers--Young Men who Woo Maturity--Old Men who Court Youth--Middle-aged Lovers.

The Question of Age.

At what age should the responsibilities of the married state be undertaken? In the best years of life if possible. Not in the physical and mental immaturity of early youth. How can the child-wife of seventeen fulfil all the duties of her position, and endow her child with the needful strength for the journey of life? How can the boy of twenty be expected to work for three without getting weary before his day has well begun? And how can either of them really know wherein true happiness lies? Most probably such a pair will learn to curse their folly before they reach maturity.

But marriage should not be shelved, and driven off to the vague period called middle-age, without excellent reason. The woman of thirty-eight and the man of forty-five will spoil their children immoderately while they are little, and be out of touch with them as they grow up. The average mother of sixty is unable to keep pace with her young daughter. The man who is nearing seventy has travelled very far away from his son who is just starting life under present-day conditions.

The Best Age.

What is a suitable disparity between the ages of man and woman? A girl of two- or three-and-twenty and a man of twenty-eight or thirty are my ideal of a suitably matched couple.

CHAPTER VII

Proposals: Premeditated, Spontaneous, Practical, or Romantic--No Rule Possible--Tact in Choosing the Opportunity--Unseemly Haste an Insult to a Woman--Keen Sense of Humour Dangerous to Sentiment--Some Things to Avoid--Vaguely Worded Offers--When She may take the Initiative.

Proposals of Marriage.

The modes of making an offer of marriage are as manifold as the minds of the men who make them. The cautious, long-headed man, whose heart is ever dominated by his head, will think out the situation carefully beforehand, and couch his offer in moderate and measured terms. The impulsive lover will be carried away by a wave of emotion, and, perhaps before he has really made up his mind, will pour out the first passionate words that come to his lips. The clear-headed business man will not lose sight of the practical advantages to be gained from the union he suggests. The creature of romance will be poetic and delightful even if utterly impossible. It may be safely said, however, that no general rule can be laid down, and that no man ever asked this important question exactly in the words or at the time he had previously selected.

Tact in Choosing the Opportunity.

The great thing is to seize the auspicious moment, to strike the responsive chord when the two minds are in harmony. A man who tries to propose when a servant is expected to arrive with a scuttle of coals, or when the children are just tumbling in from school, is not likely to meet with much {47} favour. We cannot all have the momentous question put in the witching hour of moonlight, or in the suggestive stillness of a summer's eve, but the tactful man will know when to speak, and how to turn dull prose into the sweetest rhythm.

Too Much Haste.

I do know of a case where two young people made acquaintance, wooed and married in something over a fortnight. No sane man would advocate such haste. It seems almost an impertinence for a lover to ask a woman to give herself into his keeping when he has only just made his entrance into her life. It must be admitted that Love defies time as well as locksmiths. A few hours may bring kindred souls nearer to each other than double the number of years would do in an ordinary acquaintance. On board ship, especially in the tropics, things mature with a rapidity seldom found ashore. Certain circumstances conspire to hasten the happy development, and certain conditions may justify exceptional haste. When a long separation is pending a man may be forgiven for hurrying to know his fate; but for the ordinary stay-at-home man to be introduced one week and propose the next is, to put it mildly, a doubtful compliment.

Too Keen a Sense of Humour.

A momentary realisation of the comic side of things may dash the cup of happiness from a woman's lips. An involuntary smile will be taken for heartlessness by the man who is so terribly in earnest. A humorous word will be little short of an insult, a jest but a proof of scorn. His vanity, if not his heart, will receive a wound that is not lightly to be healed. There are those who laugh from sheer nervous excitement; let them not lose the men they love by a lack of self-control that may be so cruelly misconstrued.

Some Things to Avoid.

The nervous, unready wooer both endures and inflicts agonies of mind if he tries to make a verbal offer. He had {48} much better write, for then he will at least be intelligible. The vacillating woman has no right to let a man propose to her and then accept him just because she cannot make up her mind to tell him the truth. She may mean to be kind, but she only causes unnecessary pain. No woman is justified in keeping a man in suspense while she angles for a better matrimonial prize. No honourable offer of marriage should be rejected rudely, unkindly, or with scorn. Let there be but few words spoken, but let them be simple, courteous, and, above all, definite. Let him see that you are sensible of the honour he has done you, even while you retain the right to dispose of your heart as you think best.

Vaguely Worded Offers.

It is said that the indefinite form of proposal is in favour at present. It would seem that, however he may elect to say it, the man should clearly make the lady understand that he is asking her to be his wife. She cannot very well urge him to be explicit, and, while a modest woman might thus lose her lover, an intriguing female might annex a man who had never intended to propose to her. The suitor should be quite frank as to his social position and means. It may be necessary to enter into private details of his past life. He should not conceal anything like family disgrace from the one he is asking to share his name.

Her Point of View.

A woman who loves will not need to be told how to answer her lover's request. Both lips and eyes will be eloquent without a teacher. There may be cases where a woman is justified in accepting a man for whom she only feels liking and respect, provided she has been quite frank with him, and he is content to have it so. If a man has the fidelity and pertinacity to ask a woman a second or third time he may find that the intervening years have worked in his favour; but no woman should say Yes merely because she is tired of saying No.

When She May Take the Initiative.

Old-fashioned folk say "Never." An American writer, who calls himself "A Speculative Bachelor," has quite another idea on the subject. He asks: "Shall Girls Propose?" "Why is it that in the matter of initiative a coarse, unattractive young man should have the privilege to ask any unmarried woman in the whole world to marry him, while his refined and much more accomplished sister must make no motion towards any choice of her own except to sit still and wait for some other girl's mediocre brother to make a proposal to her?"

He goes on to suggest that the practice is a survival of Asiatic barbarism. While there is no denying the truth of the above picture, it does go against the grain to think of a woman asking a man to marry her. We know that ladies of queenly rank have to do it, and lose no dignity thereby; but we are not all anxious to be royal. There is something repellent in the idea of a direct offer of marriage coming from a woman's lips. Indirectly, however, she may do much to further her own happiness.

When She May Help.

A lady of high rank may take the initiative in breaking down the barrier of social inequality which she sees is standing between her and her lover, for a man who would be held back by such a consideration would be worth bending to. The very wealthy woman, who is so often wooed for her banking account, yet is well worthy to be loved for herself, may see with secret joy that only his comparative poverty is holding back the man of her choice, and she lets love melt the golden barrier that is keeping them apart. The woman whose heart has gone out to one physically handicapped in the race with his fellows; who knows that were he as other men he would woo her with the love he is now too noble to express, surely she may take the initiative, and only gain in womanly sweetness by so doing? The woman who realises that the assurance of her love and faith will impel the man to more strenuous effort, and make his working and waiting {50}brighter for the goal that lies beyond, may be forgiven if in her intense sympathy she betray somewhat of her desire to crown his success.

A Warning.

There must be no mistake made. The wish must not be father to the thought. She must be sure that she is beloved and desired. She must throw out the most delicate feelers, so sensitive that they will at once detect coldness, and withdraw into the shell of her reserve. She must not offer herself unsought. She may not fling herself into the arms of any man's pity.

Whether there are any women who avail themselves of the supposed privilege of Leap Year, is a question that can only be answered by those who possibly prefer to keep silence. It is a questionable joke when a man says before his wife that "she married him"; but can any self-respecting woman conceive the humiliation of having such words, with the sting of truth in them, flung at her in the moment of passion or with the cool contempt of scorn?

{51}

CHAPTER VIII

Engagements--The Attitude of Parents and Guardians--Making it Known--In the Family--To Outside Friends--Congratulations--The Choice and Giving of the Ring--Making Acquaintance of Future Relations--Personally or by Letter.

Engagements.

In former days Etiquette demanded that the suitor should first make his request to the lady's parents. This may still be done with advantage in exceptional cases, notably that of a young man with his way still to make, but whose love and ambition prompt him to choose a wife from the higher social circle to which he hopes to climb. In the ordinary run of life the suitor goes first to the principal person, and when fortified by her consent bravely faces the parental music. It is not honourable for a man to make a girl an offer when he knows that her parents have a pronounced objection to him as a son-in-law. So long as she is under age, or in a dependent position, he has no right to ask her to either deceive or defy those to whom she owes duty and obedience.

The Interview.

"Asking Papa" is often a momentous matter. Some fathers are quite unreasonable, but the more honest and straightforward the suitor is the better. Let him be modest, but without cringing. There should be no suspicion that he is conferring a favour; he is rather asking a man to give him of his best, and it is his love that emboldens him to make the request.

He should state plainly what his income and prospects are, the probable date at which he will be able to marry, and how he {52} proposes to provide for his wife. He must not resent being somewhat closely questioned before his reception into a family, and should be ready to give all particulars respecting himself that may be required. Parents who value their daughter do right to exercise wise forethought before entrusting her to a comparative stranger. He should carefully avoid any unseemly curiosity as to what marriage portion his bride will have. Most men state plainly how their daughters will be dowered, unless they have reason to suspect the suitor of mercenary motives.

The father in his turn owes a measure of confidence to his child's lover, and there are some warnings that it is cruel to withhold, notably where there is any taint of insanity in the family. In the case of a fatherless girl the suitor must address himself to her mother, nearest relative, or guardian.

Refusal.

Where consent to the engagement is refused, a man of honour and good-feeling will abide by the decision, and not try to force his way into a family where he is unwelcome. He need not necessarily be fickle. Time may bring things about that will enable him, without loss of dignity, to make another and more successful attempt.

Attitude of Parents and Guardians.

Parents are often placed in great difficulties by their daughters' love affairs. They may refuse to countenance an engagement, but they cannot change the minds of the young people. On the contrary, opposition brings a sense of martyrdom which will strengthen the misplaced affection, while with judicious indifference it might have died a natural death. It is a question whether the affair shall go on in secret, nominally unknown to them, or whether they shall so far countenance it as to leave no excuse for deception. Now that so much legitimate freedom is given to girls, I cannot think that a man is acting honourably in wooing his love "under the rose," and exposing her to the matter of scandal-mongers.

Where there is nothing against a man's character or {53} antecedents, if he is able to support a wife, and the lovers are attached to each other, it seems tyrannical for parents to refuse their consent, and thus spoil their daughter's happiness.

Making it Known.

Once the engagement is ratified by the consent of the powers that be, a few days should elapse before the event is made public. The lady's parents generally give a dinner party to their most intimate friends, or an At Home if they wish to include a larger number of guests, at which the important announcement is made. The father or mother will tell the news to the most important guest or nearest relation, and it will gradually spread. Possibly the health of the happy pair may be drunk.

Friends at a Distance.

The mother of the lady writes to tell friends at a distance, but the *fiancée* would tell the good news to her own particular chums in an informal way. A motherless girl must do it all for herself. The man tells his own people and friends of his good fortune in the way that suits him best.

Congratulations.

There are many ways of offering good wishes to the engaged couple. A warm clasp of the hand and a few heartfelt words are better than all the studied elegance of phrase in the world. It is often difficult to be quite sincere in offering our congratulations, for our friends choose rather oddly, to our tastes, sometimes. When the choice of your dear friend falls on your pet abomination the case is hard indeed. You can congratulate *him*, though you want to tell him she is worlds too good for him; but what to say to *her* when you feel that she is making a disastrous match is a painful problem.

You can honestly wish that her brightest dreams may be realised, even where you have little hope of it. Let there be no bitterness in the congratulations. Respect the happiness of the lovers even if you cannot understand it.

{54}

The Ring.

In choosing the ring the lover should first think of its durability and then of its sweet symbolism. It should be the best he can afford, and the small detail of fit is not to be ignored. The choice of stones and style will depend upon taste and the money available, but, personally, I like an engagement ring to be of special design, unlike any that other women are likely to wear. One good stone is far better than a number of smaller ones.

Making Acquaintance with Future Relations.

This is one of the bride-elect's sorest trials, for even when people like a girl very well as a friend, they do not always welcome her as a member of their family. She must face the fact that they have not chosen her, and the more simply and naturally she bears herself under the inevitable criticism the better. It is fatal to *try* and make a good impression. Tact and intuition will do a great deal for her, but much lies in the power of his relations to make or mar the happiness of her entry into their midst. I know of a girl, who lived a long way from her *fiancé*, who was made quite miserable during her occasional visits to his home by the discourtesy of his sisters. He was in town all day, and of course knew nothing of the discomfort she endured in his absence. He knows now, and it has not increased his brotherly love.

What She Should Avoid.

It is bad manners in a girl to try and show off her power over her lover in his own home, or anywhere else, for the matter of that. It is foolish to pretend that she does not care for him, or to talk of her wedding-day as if it were her execution. I have known girls who did this. She should not devote herself exclusively to him, and thereby fail in courtesy to his family or their friends. She should not boast of her own people, or infer that her home is superior to theirs. She should guard especially against anything that looks like wishing to oust her lover's mother from her place in his affections. Women are nearly always a little jealous of the girls their sons marry, and care must be taken to disarm this.

Letters.

When the introductions take place mainly by letter, many stumbling-blocks are removed from the path of the bride-elect. It only behoves her to reply with ready, grateful recognition to the words of welcome, which should be gracious and warm-hearted on the part of his friends. The following may serve as an example:--

From his Mother

"My dear Sybil,--Frank has told me of his engagement to you, and I am writing to tell you how glad I am and how fully I enter into his happiness. I feel sure, my dear child, that he will make you a good and loving husband, for he has been such a dear son to me.

"I have always prayed that he might find a wife who would appreciate his love and share his highest interests. I am now satisfied that he has done this, dear. I want you to come and stay with me as soon as you can, so that we may learn to understand each other. It ought not to be difficult, now that we have so much in common.--With kind love, believe me, affectionately yours,   Alice Stanley."

The above letter would imply that the mother knew a good deal about the girl her son was going to marry, and of course she would try to write in a cordial strain, even though she was taking her future daughter-in-law upon the son's recommendation.

The girl's answer might be on these lines:--

"My dear Mrs. Stanley,--You cannot think how glad I was to receive your most kind letter. It is such a relief to feel that you do not disapprove of Frank's choice. I only hope that you may still approve when you know me better. I am delighted to accept your kind invitation, and can come on the 14th if that will suit you. I can hardly yet realise my great happiness, and feel that I can never do enough for Frank.--With many thanks for your kindness, believe me, with love, yours affectionately, Sybil Carlton."

CHAPTER IX

His Visits to her Home--The Engaged Couple in Public--In Society--Visiting at the same House--Going about together--The Question of Expenses.

His Visits to her Home.

If distance parts the loving couple he will only be able to spend his leave, or annual holidays, with her, and will make a point of consulting her movements before he lays any plans for his leisure time. If he could meet her abroad, or at the seaside, he would not go off yachting without her, nor postpone his holiday till the shooting had begun rather than spend the month of June with her in the suburbs. If he lives in the same neighbourhood as his beloved he will have many opportunities of being with her. He ought never to neglect his work for his courtship, and a girl should be very careful not to propose such a thing. It is a poor lookout for their future if they put pleasure first. He will probably be expected or permitted to spend two or three evenings a week at her home, dine there on Sundays, and, if he is busy all the week, devote Saturday afternoons to her entirely. A man of leisure can make his own arrangements; the business or professional man must do his love-making when he can.

The Engaged Couple in Public.

"Some men like to advertise their kissing rights," said an engaged man to me the other day; "but for my part I don't think there should be anything in the bearing of an engaged couple in public to indicate that they are more than friends." Here, I think, we have the etiquette of the matter in a nutshell. Wherever the lovers are they will be supremely conscious of each other's presence, but it need not be writ {57} large over their actions. It is sometimes debated whether lovers should kiss in public. As the sweetest kisses must ever be those exchanged "under four eyes," as the Germans put it, there seems little advantage in a mere conventional "peck" in the public gaze. A close clasp of the hand, a silent greeting of the eyes, will be truer to the love that is held too sacred for exhibition.

The man's attentions should never merge into questionable hilarity. He ought to respect as well as love the woman he hopes to marry. She should equally avoid gushing and tyrannising over him. To see a girl ordering her *fiancé* about, making him fetch and carry like a black boy, and taking his submission as her due, is enough to justify the hope that the worm will turn to some purpose when she least expects it. There should be nothing abject in love on either side. It hurts to see the dog-like look of entreaty in human eyes. Things should be more on a level; the hearts of man and woman should give and take gladly of their best, with love that is pure, brave, and unashamed.

In Society.

Mutual friends will be sure to invite the engaged couple to various social functions. Where it is possible and convenient they will arrive and leave together. He will naturally be eager to escort her about as much as he can; they must, however, be prepared to sacrifice themselves on such occasions. He will see that she has all she wants at a garden party or At Home, but he will not glare at another man for handing her an ice or a cup of tea; nor will he neglect his duties to sit in his sweetheart's pocket, or stand behind her chair to warn off intruders. On the other hand he will not attract attention by devoting himself to any one particular lady, or play into the hands of the wanton flirt.

A well-bred woman or girl will not give herself away by allowing awkward pauses to break the conversation because her thoughts and eyes are hungrily trying to follow her lover, who is manfully assisting the hostess. She will not make herself conspicuous in her behaviour with any other admirer, but be perfectly at ease with any man to whom she may have occasion to speak.

If any of the lady's friends wish to make her *fiancé's* acquaintance they will send him an invitation to a dance or party through her, not an informal message, but a card such as they send to their other guests, which she will pass on to him.

{58}

Visiting at the same House.

The engaged couple are not considered good company by outsiders, so when they are included in a house-party they should exercise a little healthful self-control. The cosy corners, shady walks, and secluded nooks are not their monopoly. The two who are beginning to make love ought to have a chance. Others may have business to discuss, arrangements to make, or letters to write for which they desire privacy, and the pervading presence of the betrothed pair is apt to become irritating. When etiquette requires that they should be parted, it is their duty to fall in courteously with any arrangement their hostess may make.

Going about Together.

The amount of *tête-à-tête* intercourse will differ in almost every case. It seems most natural that lovers should go about together as much as possible, seeing that they are learning to pass their lives together. The girl who has taken little expeditions with her *fiancé* will be spared much of the embarrassment that might mar the opening of the honeymoon if she felt shy and strange, cut off from all her old moorings. They will spend long days on the river, take rambles into the country, see the sights of the town, and do a hundred other things that will be doubly delightful just because they are alone together.

The Question of Expenses.

It is sometimes taken for granted that the *fiancé* must pay all expenses when he takes his sweetheart about. This, I think, should depend upon circumstances. The rich lover does well to lavish his money upon his future wife, and will {59} take a pride in so doing. The man of moderate means who has to work for his income will do well to put by all he can for future emergencies, and if the girl to whom he is engaged has her own money or an ample allowance, it is much better that they should come to an understanding to share the cost of their pleasures, in view of possible necessities.

This need not prevent the poorer man from spending a certain amount upon his love. Every now and then there will be special days when he will play the host, and they will be red-letter days to both. If she is going anywhere by his special invitation he would naturally defray her expenses; but on their weekly jaunts why should he be put to the double outlay when he wants to save all he can to start their home? Why should he reduce his balance at the bank by first-class fares, theatre tickets, and taxis two or three times a week, when he may have to borrow money to buy their furniture? No girl ought to expect or encourage this sort of thing. She is not afraid of being under an obligation to him, for love knows no such thing, but she has the wisdom to look ahead.

CHAPTER X

Love-Letters--Long or Short Engagements--Broken Engagements--Clandestine Engagements--When Justifiable--The Mother in the Secret--Friends who act as Go-Between.

Love-Letters.

There are, I believe, engaged couples who, after parting from each other at 7 P.M., write a long letter before going to bed that night, containing all that they had not time to say. If they have the time and energy to spare it concerns no one but themselves; but it seems a pity to make a rule of this sort, as it may become a tax, and the breaking of it on either side may cause pain if not friction.

There will be times without number when delightful little love-letters will have to be written. They will come as a joyful surprise and be twice as sweet as those that are expected.

When daily or even frequent meetings are impossible, then the love-letter has a most important part to play in the course of true love. Letters are a very valuable addition to personal intercourse. It is not safe to judge a person entirely from them, but taking them side by side with personal knowledge they throw a good deal of light on a character. The glamour of the beloved presence is not there to blind, the charm of manner or voice is not powerful to fascinate, so the words stand on their own merits. Sometimes they do not quite fit in with what we know of the writer. They show us another side of one we love. It may be endearing, it may be the reverse. In any case the letters that pass between an engaged couple should be kept absolutely private. We know the story of the man who wrote the same love-letters to two girls, who {61} discovered his treachery by comparing their respective treasures. Such a case is, I hope, purely fictional, but there ought to be some exceptionally good reason for divulging the sweet nothings that go to make up the typical love-letter. For the one to whom they are addressed they will be sublime, to the outsider they will probably be only ridiculous.

The Length of Engagements.

Considering what a vital change marriage is bound to bring into the lives of those who make the contract, it would seem the height of rashness to hurry into it with a person of whom one knows but little. It may be contended that the mutual attitude of lovers during their engagement is not calculated to enlarge their real knowledge of each other. Certainly not, if the marriage is to take place while they are at fever-heat, living in a whirl of emotional rapture. But let an engagement be long enough for their love to settle down into a more normal state, where their reasoning faculties will be able to work--then they will gain a clearer estimate of their mutual fitness, and may learn a good deal about each other.

It has been said that no man should make an offer of marriage till he is in a position to support a wife. This is a little hard. If a man is worth having, he is worth waiting for. He has no right to speak till he has some definite prospect in view, or unless he is fully determined to do his best to further his own interests. No girl or woman should be expected to waste her youth and wear out her heart as the promised wife of a man who is not trying to make their marriage possible. Above all, no man should be mean enough to take money from the one to whom he is engaged merely to indulge his own idleness.

A year or eighteen months may be taken as a fair time for the engagement of those who have known but little of each other beforehand. In the case of long intimacy six months will probably suffice. A girl exposes herself to much unpleasant criticism by urging on a hasty marriage. Even if she feels impatient, she should let that sort of thing come from the man. If he lets the time drag on with seeming {62} indifference or satisfaction, she should ask one of her parents to speak to him on the subject, and if she guesses that he has no real desire to marry her, she had far better give him up altogether than urge him to take the step unwillingly.

Broken Engagements.

It sometimes happens that during this period of courtship either the man or the woman realises that a mistake has been made; if so, let it be rectified before a still more serious one be committed. It is a delicate matter for a man to take the initiative. No woman should drive him to do so. Let her make him a present of his freedom before he has to ask for it. It is due to a man's self-respect to break with a woman who openly and wantonly disregards his wishes on any important point. In the same way if a man will not give up bad habits, such as gambling, intemperance, or whatever it may be, for the sake of the girl he is engaged to, she may be pretty sure that he will not do it when she is his wife. Let him choose between her and his vices.

Once the engagement is at an end the ring and other presents should be sent back, unless by special mutual arrangement to the contrary. Letters are either burnt or returned to the writer. There is a good deal of sentiment about these written proofs of a love that has proved a failure, on one side at least. The two who have been so nearly one now become mere acquaintances again in the eyes of the world, and will probably not be anxious to meet for some time to come.

Clandestine Engagement.

The obstacle to true love in former days was parental authority, which often savoured of tyranny. In these days of liberty the young people have it more their own way. When parents object to a lover on the mere ground of his poverty, or some personal prejudice, a girl may be excused for making her own choice when she is of age. If she binds herself secretly to a man whose moral unfitness is objected to, she is courting certain misery and possible disgrace.

A Justifiable Case.

It would seem, then, that where parental consent is refused on the ground of advisability, not of vital principle, the girl is justified in holding herself bound till such time as she is free to give her hand in marriage. She will use this bond as a defence against other suitors who may be urged upon her. She will not flaunt her decision in the parental face, nor cause ructions by tactlessly obtruding the bone of contention; but she will be firm and loyal, true to herself and to him she loves.

Where the Mother Shares the Secret.

Where the father is somewhat of a Spartan there is not unfrequently a gentle, sympathetic mother, who will dare much to make her child happy. The daughter is well advised to make such a mother her confidante. A woman who schemes to entangle a young man of wealth or high rank into a secret engagement with her daughter, who she knows is no suitable wife for him, is neither honest to him nor kind to her child. Such unequal marriages seldom answer in real life. There must be sympathy, and a certain community of interests to make marriage a success.

Friends who act as Go-Between.

There is a spice of romance in helping distressed and persecuted lovers; but young people should be very careful not to mix themselves up in such matters. Their own experience is too limited to qualify them for the task. Older friends must take the consequences of such interference. Sometimes their help is most ill-advised; still, for a time at least, the lovers will be intensely grateful to them. There is one thing that seems quite unjustifiable, and that is for a secretly engaged pair to make a friend's house their rendezvous without telling the friend exactly how matters stand. It is an abuse of hospitality, for it is pretty sure to bring unpleasantness to the friend, who will inevitably be blamed by the parents when the secret leaks out, or an elopement takes {64} place. Trains, telephones, and telegraphs have robbed the latter episode of all its old-world reckless charm, and it really seems hardly worth the doing.

In some cases a married friend may intervene to prevent any scandal from touching the wilful bride. If the young folks will not listen to reason, it is as well for their folly to be carried out as respectably as possible; but all such sympathy should be tempered by judgment, for the making or marring of two lives is in the balance, and the happiness of many hearts may be at stake.

CHAPTER XI

Foreign Etiquette of Engagements--Betrothal a much more Serious Matter than in England.

In no other country is an engagement so informal as in England. We find all sorts of ceremonies connected with the plighting of a troth which seems but little less important than the tying of the marriage knot itself. There is less spontaneity and exercise of private judgment on the part of the young people; in fact, there are several countries in which they are allowed no voice in the matter.

In Italy

girls are kept quite in the background, and have a very dull time. This makes them ready to accept any suitor their parents may choose. A meeting is arranged between the young people, and after that he pays stiff visits to her home, generally in the evening, but they are never left alone together, and he is not allowed to pay her any marked attention even before others. They may exchange photographs, and she may work him a little present; but it is all lifeless, passionless, and business-like. Among the peasantry there is more of the picturesque, and many quaint customs still survive. Marriage-brokers do a good trade, and get a percentage on each pair that they see through the ordeal of a wedding. In Frascati, parents with marriageable sons and daughters assemble on Sunday afternoons in the chief piazza. The men sit on one side and the women on the other. In the intervening space the candidates for matrimony walk about--the girls near their mothers, the youths under their fathers' eyes. By some mysterious process of selection they sort themselves into couples, or, rather, the parents make mutual advances on behalf of their children and they are betrothed.

In France

similar restrictions are placed upon lovers, and no one under the age of twenty-five can contract a legal marriage without the consent of his or her parents. If three appeals have been made in vain for parental sanction, there may be an appeal to the law. The proposed marriage must also be publicly announced beforehand, or it is invalid. In *Brittany* there is a strange mixture of the romantic and the practical. The village tailor is the usual negotiator who interviews both the lovers and their parents. When he has smoothed the way, the intending bridegroom pays his first visit, which is accompanied by many pretty customs. He is allowed to take his sweetheart aside, and no one dares to interrupt this, their first, *tête-à-tête*. Meanwhile the elders discuss business, and when the lovers come back to the family circle a feast is enjoyed, at which the parents bless the food, and the lovers are only allowed one knife and plate between them. The signing of the wedding contract later on is another festivity, and the presents are mostly of a useful nature.

German Betrothals

are more or less formal, though the young couple are allowed to choose for themselves. The suitor has not much chance of seeing the lady alone before he has made up his mind; he must be circumspect, or his intentions will be promptly inquired into. He puts on his Sunday clothes with lavender kids when he comes to ask the important question, and as soon as a satisfactory answer has been obtained the happy pair are congratulated by the family, and the table is decorated for the festive meal. They go out arm-in-arm to call upon their friends in a day or two, and a formal announcement is not only sent round to all their acquaintance, but is also inserted in the daily papers. Great attention must be paid to the exact title possessed by every one connected with the happy pair, as titles count for much in Germany. The engaged girl is called a bride, and her lover a bridegroom, before marriage. She shows her prowess in the culinary line by preparing the meals to which he is invited. They are not supposed to travel alone; even if they are going to stay with his relations, some lady must {67} accompany them. In many cases the parents have qualms about allowing too much *tête-à-tête* intercourse to the engaged couple, but greater liberty is gradually being given.

In Russia

it is considered a disgrace for a woman to be unmarried, and if no suitor offers himself, she leaves her home and settles in a strange place as a widow. She may prefer to travel for a time, and return home with a pitiful tale of the husband she lost at sea, or who died at the beginning of the honeymoon. The priests often act as intermediaries, but sometimes a woman versed in dark lore makes the arrangements. At the betrothal feast the girl gives her lover a long lock of her hair, and he gives her a silver ring set with turquoise, bread and salt, and an almond cake. This interchange of gifts is equal to a marriage bond. All the presents have a symbolical meaning; the rings are bought from and blessed by the clergy, and are treasured as heirlooms in the family.

In Spain

girls are most jealously guarded, and marriages are arranged by the parents. Still the romantic element is not wanting. The young man sees the lady who steals his heart, and begins to woo her from a distance with eyes and voice till he can gain an introduction to her family. The main joy in a Spanish courtship is the clandestine prelude to the actual engagement. He may follow the lady about and serenade her, according to regulations, but he may not speak till he is introduced. She appears to ignore his attentions, but she misses nothing. The courtship is often protracted, but the girl is given freedom of choice. The law can come to the assistance of lovers whose union is prevented by their parents, in the same way as in France.

The amount of liberty given to the engaged couple differs in various districts, but throughout Spain the love making may be said to end with marriage. In Murcia they may not meet or speak unless her mother is present, and the lover may neither touch the hand nor kiss the lips of his sweetheart till she is his wife.

{68}

Sweden.

Unmarried girls in this country enjoy an unrivalled reputation for gaiety and merriment. Bread is considered a love charm, and the two who eat from the same loaf will fall in love with each other. The suitor often sends an ambassador to a girl he has never seen, and if his proposal is accepted he calls the next Sunday. The lady is not supposed to take any notice of him, but continues her knitting in a stolid fashion. In some parts there is a religious betrothal ceremony, when plain gold rings are exchanged; but the more usual way of celebrating an engagement is by a social festivity. The lover must give a "Yes-Gift" to his future bride, which consists of a gold or silver cup--the size is not stipulated--filled with coins wrapped up in quite new white tissue-paper. He also gives her a prayer-book, while she offers in return some garment she has made for him herself. If it is a shirt he wears it on his wedding-day, and then lays it aside to wear in his grave. These quaint customs are mostly found in the country districts. Town-dwellers merely send out cards with the names of the pair printed on each one, and further announcements appear in the papers.

In Switzerland

there is not much romance in either wooing or wedding. The Swiss may not marry till the youth is eighteen and the girl sixteen, and up to the age of twenty the consent of parents or guardians is necessary. When the time draws near for the wedding, the pair must go together to a civil officer, and must each present him with a certificate of birth, and tell him their ages, names, professions, and where they and where their parents live. He then writes a deed containing their promise of marriage, which must be made public for at least a fortnight in the places where they were born, where they are living at the time, and where they wish to be married. If nobody makes an objection the ceremony can take place. May-Day is sacred to lovers in Lucerne. He plants a small decorated pine-tree before her house at dawn, and if he is accepted a right royal feast is prepared for him. The little tree is {69} treasured till the first baby appears. A Swiss peasant girl is often compelled to take the lover who lives nearest to her home, as the introduction of an outsider is resented by the men of the place.

The Hungarian

likes to linger over his wooing, and he is a past master in the art. The lovers have absolute freedom of intercourse, and secure privacy in the family circle by making a tent of his large, graceful cloak, under which they sit and make love undisturbed. All the actual formalities go through a third person, and much ceremony is observed in the negotiations. The first stage of courtship is marked by the "Loving Cup" feast, and the binding betrothal is known as the "Kissing Feast."

In Norway

courtship is of necessity a very long process among the peasant folk, for money is not easily earned, and no man may marry till he is a householder, while houses may only be built in certain places and under fixed regulations. Seven years is quite an average time for an engagement, during which they do their love-making in a simple, unaffected manner. No man ever jilts a woman, and broken engagements are almost unknown.

In *Greece* parents pay a man to marry their daughter, and no man may marry till all his own sisters are provided with *trousseaux* and dowers.

The girl who *accepts* an offer of marriage in *Greenland* is for ever disgraced. Her father may give her away or her husband may drag her by her hair to his own tent, and it is all right. She must be married by capture, against her own will, and the love comes afterwards, if at all.

A Thuringian girl gives her suitor sausage to eat as a sign that he is rejected. A Spanish maid presents her lover with a pumpkin as her way of saying "No." In the Russian district of the Ukraine the lady does the courting, and {70} besieges the man in his own house. Courtesy will not let him turn her out, so if he does not want her he has to seek other quarters for himself. On the Isthmus of Darien either man or woman can take the initiative, so every one gets a good chance all round.

It is not possible, here, to touch upon the elaborate betrothal and marriage customs of the East.

{71}

CHAPTER XII

Marriage--Fixing the Day--Preparations--Selecting the Bridesmaids and their Dresses--The Wedding Gown--The Trousseau--Invitations.

Marriage.

The aim of all true Courtship is marriage, which should take place as soon as an engagement has lasted long enough to serve its purpose, and when other circumstances are propitious. When the man's financial position is sufficiently secured, and the woman is willing to renounce her freedom for bonds that should be blessed, he asks her to "name the happy day."

Fixing the Day.

In foreign countries there are many superstitions as to the fitness or unfitness of days, times, and seasons; but in England May appears to be the only month supposed to be unlucky for weddings. The reason for this does not seem clear. The couplet

"If married in Lent

You are sure to repent,"

is an echo from the days when Church discipline was stricter than it is now, and the time set apart for spiritual sorrow was not considered suitable for the crowning of earthly happiness. Even in the present day very few marriages are celebrated during the season of Lent.

There are many people and things to take into account when fixing the important date. If the bridegroom elect is not his own master a time must be chosen when he is sure to be at liberty. It was said of the late Sir Walter

Besant {72} that he was so overwhelmed with business that he hardly had time to be married. The bride's father has also to be considered, and if any particular church dignitary is required to perform the ceremony his engagements will have to be taken into account.

When possible it is well to let a good interval elapse between the final decision and the day itself. A month or six weeks is none too much; more than this is often allowed.

The Bride's Burden.

There is a great deal of mental wear and tear for the bride-elect to go through in the few weeks immediately before her marriage, and it is a pity that it should be so. The fuss and display at an up-to-date wedding make it a thing to quail before. Dress has become so extravagant and absorbing that in the matter of her clothes alone the girl has her time pretty well taken up. Instead of being able to prepare calmly and restfully for the most vital step in life, she is kept in a ceaseless whirl of mental and physical excitement till she is well-nigh worn out. In any case care should be taken to avoid a rush at the last. Let her have at least a few days of peace and quietness in which to prepare for the great event. How can she realise the solemnity of the vows she is going to make, or the gravity of the responsibility she is taking upon her shoulders, if she never has a moment to think and is being hurried from milliner to dressmaker, from jeweller to shoemaker, from furrier to glovemaker, day in day out?

The Choice of the Bridesmaids.

In some families this is a difficult matter, and may be the cause of much friction. The bride's sisters, if she has any, take precedence. There may be a dear friend who has been promised this office since she and the bride were at school together, but then *his* sisters expect to be asked, and they may be neither attractive nor very young. When the desired number is but small, the problem is sometimes solved by having two or three children and forswearing all adults. This is certainly a prettier and less expensive arrangement, for children look more picturesque as bridesmaids than the {73} average half-dozen grown-up girls who cannot be chosen for their appearance. Elderly bridesmaids in youthful frocks and girlish hats are ridiculous to the unthinking, but pathetic to those who look below the surface.

Wedding Frocks.

"Married in white you have chosen all right," says the old rhyme, and the "ivory duchesse satin" seems to have come to stay. There should, however, be some regard for the future social position of the bride in choosing the wedding gown. The girl who is marrying a man with a small income, and who is prepared to begin housekeeping on a simple scale, is not likely to want a magnificent satin dinner-gown with a court train. A much less expensive frock would answer her requirements far better, for, with the ever-changing fashions, the costly material would have to be cut up and altered many a time before it was worn out. It is a pity to weigh down a young girlish bride with heavy brocades and silks that stand alone. Her freshness and beauty will stand a simpler setting, and look all the sweeter in it. There are so many soft, diaphanous fabrics made now, which fall into graceful draperies, that I would like the young bride clad in some of them.

The Bridesmaids' Dresses.

The choice of a costume for the bridesmaids is not an easy matter. You can find one that will suit two sisters to perfection, but there are the others, with possibly such colouring as to forbid the very thing that another will look her best in. White is taken as being generally safe and becoming, but when worn unrelieved in the daytime it is very trying to some. There are also the height and build of the various girls to be considered, so altogether the matter demands much care and taste.

Expense.

The question of cost should not be ignored unless the bride is in a position to give all the dresses, then she may be as lavish as she thinks fit.

It is hardly fair to expect her friends to go to the most {74} expensive house and to buy the most costly hats and frocks, which will perhaps be of little use to them afterwards, merely for her personal gratification. This is especially the case where two sisters are asked to be bridesmaids. A girl may long to attend her friend to the altar, and yet be obliged to decline because her parents cannot afford the outlay necessitated by the extravagance of the costume. If one has her frock made by an artiste, the others must follow suit or the picture is spoilt.

The bride who is married in her travelling dress does not have bridesmaids but attendants, whose dresses should harmonise but not eclipse her own. Due regard should be paid to the time of year in the choice of materials. White gauzy frocks look chill and comfortless in mid-winter, even if the wearers do not shiver perceptibly and are not afflicted with red noses; but soft, thick fabrics like white cloth or velvet trimmed with touches of fur, suggest the warmth that lies beneath the snow. The flowers of the season may well provide schemes of colour, for Nature is the prince of artists. Primrose and daffodil tints for the spring, the warm tones of the chrysanthemum for the autumn, while summer sunshine makes everything look well.

The Trousseau.

A young friend of mine who was going to be married last year said to me: "Oh! my things are so lovely! I never knew how delightful it was to be able to have all the beautiful things you want." This sentiment will be echoed by most of the fairly-well dowered brides of to-day. There is generally a fixed sum set apart for the trousseau, and the amount must necessarily control the extent of the purchases. The *lingerie* and underwear can be obtained from about ten guineas, with prices varying according to the number and quality of the garments, up to forty or fifty guineas. Dresses, boots and shoes, and all out-door wear, including hats, must be added on to this outlay.

Few people buy many dresses at once now, on account of the changeful whims of fashion; but the great point is to have the few gowns of good material and excellent cut.

There are a hundred items, only known to a woman {75} or her maid, with which the bride should be well stocked. It is a disgrace to don a costly opera-cloak when you have not a decent dressing-gown, or to load yourself with finery when your stockings are in holes. Feminine attire is so dainty and fascinating in the present day that there is a danger of setting more value on the trimmings and make than on the quality of the material. Let the bride-elect try to picture her pretty things when they emerge from the ruthless hands of a laundress, and she will realise the value of quality. Where anything like regular or hard wear is required, it is always good economy to buy the best. All garments that need to be marked must have the initials of the bride's married name upon them. All women are supposed to love shopping. Surely no expeditions can be so delightful as going to buy the trousseau with a well-stocked purse!

Invitations.

These are sent out by the bride's mother, or whoever acts in that capacity. Any good stationer will have plenty of printed cards, such as are generally used, from which a choice may be made. Simplicity of design is always a mark of refinement. The wording would be as follows:

Mr. and Mrs. Carstairs

request the pleasure of

Captain and Mrs. Boyd's company

at

the Marriage of their Daughter

Gladys

with

Mr. Sydney Boroughs,

at

S. John's, Beckenham,

on Wednesday, April 17th, at 2 p.m.,

and afterwards at the Grange.

R.S.V.P.

Any friend who has sent a present before the invitations are out must be invited. The general feeling seems to be that {76} an invitation to a wedding involves a present, and that is rather a tax. It also takes away from that purely voluntary spirit which is the beauty of a gift. In some cases friends are only asked to the church, the reception at home being confined to members of the two families.

A bridesmaid who lives at a distance must be asked to stay at the bride's home for a few days before the wedding.

The death of a near relation would necessitate the postponement of the wedding, and this would cancel all invitations. In cases of loss more remote from the young couple, the wedding takes place soon after the first date, "but quietly, owing to family bereavement." A notice to this effect is often put in the papers when a marriage has been publicly announced, but in a more private affair, notes would be sent to those who had been invited.

{77}

CHAPTER XIII

Wedding Presents--Choosing and Furnishing the House--What the Bridegroom Supplies--The Bride's Share in the Matter.

Wedding Presents.

With the increasing luxury and love of display that marks modern life the wedding-present tax, as I have heard it called, becomes a burden proportionately heavy to the social ambition of the giver. It seems a pity that there should be so much vulgarising advertisement about what are supposed to be private weddings. There is also too much routine in the choice of the gifts themselves. The perennial mustard-pots and salt-cellars are monotonous, and while comparative strangers may be driven to make a conventional offering, private friends might leave the groove and strike out a new line.

Cheques are only given by old friends or relations of the recipient. They are always acceptable. The future position of the couple should be taken into account. Good silver is always a joy, except perhaps when you have to keep it clean. The young wife with only one servant will have to rub up her own silver backed brushes and sweetmeat dishes if she wants them to look nice. Of course it may be said that extra silver can be put by till circumstances improve, or that it might be useful in a financial emergency. This last idea is rather a gruesome one to take to a wedding, and it is in the early days of her housekeeping that the young wife likes to have her pretty things about her. Why an artistic chair or table should not be as suitable as an *entrée dish* I do not quite see, and if a place is to look homelike pictures are quite as necessary as silver pepper-pots.

A Temptation.

Both bride and bridegroom receive presents, some for individual, others for mutual use. The bride must promptly and personally acknowledge all those that are sent to her, and the bridegroom does the same on his own account. Presents from mutual friends would be mutually acknowledged, especially if the gift were sent to both of them. When one does not feel very kindly disposed to the man or woman whom our dear friend is going to marry there is a great temptation--I don't know that it need be resisted--to send a gift that will be the property and pleasure of that friend, and not to give the mutual mustard-pot into which both will dip the spoon.

How to Send Them.

All wedding presents should be nicely and daintily packed up. Sometimes they are better sent from the shop direct, but in that case the card or cards of the donors should accompany them. Many people tie their cards on with narrow white ribbon, and anything that adds to the daintiness of a present is to be commended. It is a very sensible plan for relations to let the young people choose their own sideboard or dinner service, instead of buying it for them. There is only one drawback to this arrangement. The thing that costs the most is so often the thing we want most, even before we know the price, and it would not be nice to feel we had trespassed on the generosity of the giver by inducing him to spend more than he intended. It is becoming the fashion for members of a family to club together and give a handsome piece of jewellery, instead of each one presenting a smaller trinket. This might well be done with more practical presents.

The Art of Giving.

Much of the pleasure afforded by a gift is contained in the way it is given. There is an exquisite art in giving. Many people choose a present just because they happen to like the thing themselves, whereas a gift should be selected entirely with a view to the pleasure or use it will afford to its future owner. A grand piano is no good to a girl who will not have {79} a room large enough to hold it and herself. Costly china is only an encumbrance to a woman who is going to follow the fortunes of her soldier husband, and who will not have a settled home for years. There must be kindly sympathy in the choice of gifts as well as tact and courtesy in the offering of them.

The Selection of the House.

Whenever it is possible the young or newly married couple should start their life together in a home of their own. I would warn all brides to superintend the choice of that home. A man, certainly one of the nicest kind, has not what may be called a domestic eye. If he is artistic he will choose a dwelling for its picturesqueness, regardless of drains and dank ditches near the house. An inert man will value his home for its proximity to the station. Another considers the garden the most important feature. The stay-at-home will be influenced by the place which affords the most scope for the pursuit of his hobbies. Men cannot gauge the amount of work that may be made or saved by the build of a house and the arrangement of its rooms. The all-important question of cupboards and store-rooms, the aspect of the larder and condition of the kitchen range are things that do not appeal to the masculine mind, especially when that mind is in love. If the bride is young and inexperienced she will do well to visit the projected abode with some practised housewife. The expeditions taken by the engaged couple in search of their new home ought surely to be among their sweetest experiences, even taking into account the misleading tactics of the house agent.

Furnishing.

In olden days, when the daughters of Eve span, the bride provided all the household linen, most of which had taken shape under her own fair fingers. Now the intending bridegroom furnishes the house throughout. If the bride's father were wealthy and generous enough to make them a present of the lining for the nest, I do not suppose the bridegroom or the bride would have any objection. One argument for not furnishing till after the wedding is that many of the presents in money and kind might be valuable adjuncts; {80} but then those presents would come from near relations who could tell the young people what to expect. A chest of plate or a box of linen, a piano or some such handsome item often comes from some one in the bride's family, but failing such gifts, the bridegroom must supply the new home with all needful articles.

The Bride's Share in the Matter.

As she is to be the mistress of the establishment, the bride should have a voice in all that concerns it. Many departments of house furnishing do not require the assistance of the male mind at all. They will both like to choose the actual household gods, to discuss schemes of colour and decoration together; but no woman need take a man to buy saucepans, or request his opinion on such soft matters as pillows and blankets. It will please his mother if the bride consults her about domestic details, and in any case she will profit by the advice of one who has been there.

Things to be Considered.

However small it is, the newly married pair should have their home to themselves, and it is as well not to settle immediately under the parental eye on either side. Like Kipling's ship, they have to "find themselves," and they will do it far better alone together. At the same time it is not good for a bride to be set down in an utterly strange neighbourhood, where she will not know a soul till the people are thoroughly satisfied as to her respectability. This, as we shall see later, may constitute a grave danger.

The husband should think of his wife's daily round as well as of his own train service to town or the house's proximity to the golf links. They should go to some place within easy reach of friends, or where they have good introductions to possible people. When preparing to start life together they should not be too ambitious. Because she has been brought up in a big house, he is doing her no kindness by saddling himself with a higher rent than he can really afford to pay. She is quite willing to take him in exchange for the extra accommodation that she is giving up. That is, if she is the right sort of woman.

CHAPTER XIV

The Nature of the Ceremony--Religious or Civil--Banns or Licence--Legal Formalities--Settlements.

The Nature of the Ceremony.

In most foreign countries a civil contract has to precede any religious ceremony that may be desired. In England the marriage is either religious or civil, though in order to make the union valid certain legal formalities must be observed with every religious form of marriage.

The Religious Ceremony

will not lightly be set aside by those who regard marriage in its highest aspect; but the nature of the service will differ according to the views of the contracting parties. A valid marriage can only take place in a church or chapel duly licensed by the bishop for the solemnisation of such a ceremony.

Banns.

This word, which we now connect exclusively with the one idea, applied in former days to any public proclamation. Where marriage by banns is desired due notice must be given, so that they can be published on three Sundays, before the ceremony, in the parish or parishes where the intending bride and bridegroom live at the time. If the wedding is to take place elsewhere the clergyman who has published the banns signs a certificate to that effect, which must be given to the one in whose church the service is performed. If wrong names are wilfully given in, with intent to deceive, the publication of banns is invalid, and the marriage will be null and void. If only one party be guilty of fraud in this respect the proceedings are legal. Unless the couple are married within three months of the publication of their banns they must be republished or a licence procured. One object of these restrictions is to check runaway matches, and to ascertain whether the parties are of legal age, or are marrying with proper consent from parents or guardians. A marriage may be performed in a church without banns on production of a registrar's certificate. I know of a runaway couple who were married in church as soon as their parents found out that they had been before the registrar.

Licences.

These are of two kinds, the common and the special. A common licence is given by the archbishop or bishop, and can be obtained in London at the Faculty Office, 23 Knightrider's Street, Doctors' Commons, E.C., or at the Vicar-General's Office, 3 Creed Lane, Ludgate Hill, E.C., between the hours of 10 A.M. and 4 P.M., on all week days, except Saturday, when they close at 2 P.M. Licences from these two places are available for use in any part of England or Wales. They cost thirty shillings, with an extra twelve and sixpence for stamps. In order to prevent fraud, no licence can be given till one of the parties has made a declaration on oath that there is no legal impediment to the marriage, and that one of them has lived for fifteen days in the parish or district where the wedding is to take place. This last restriction is often evaded by the bridegroom's taking a bedroom in which he possibly sleeps one night, and where he is represented by a bag containing--stones, or a collar, if he likes.

Those licences obtained from the bishop's diocesan registry can only be used in the diocese where they are issued. They cost from £1, 15s. to £2, 12s. 6d., according to the diocese. The vicar or rector of any parish will give full particulars as to how they are to be obtained in country places.

The Special Licence

costs about £30, and is given by the archbishop through the Faculty Office under certain conditions. It dispenses with {83} previous residence in the district, and can be used anywhere and at any time, providing satisfactory reasons have been given for its issue.

Witnesses.

No marriage should be performed in any church or chapel unless at least two witnesses are present, who also attest the signing of the parish register. The ordinary fee for the certificate, or "marriage lines," is 2s. 7d., including the stamp, but this charge may vary a little.

The Civil Contract.

This may be done by certificate or licence. If a certificate is required, one of the parties must give formal notice to the superintendent registrar of the district in which both have lived for seven days immediately preceding the notice. If the couple live in separate places, similar notice must be given by each one. A solemn statement that there is no legal obstacle to the marriage must be made, together with notification of their places of residence, and, in the case of a minor, whether the consent of parent or guardian is forthcoming. The certificate may not be issued for twenty-one days after the notice has been entered, and this certificate is only available for three months.

After the expiration of twenty-one days the wedding may take place at the Registry Office, in the presence of the superintendent registrar, a registrar of the district, and two witnesses, within the appointed hours, from 8 A.M. to 3 P.M. The mutual declaration is short and to the point. A ring is usually employed, but I have heard of strange substitutes being used at a pinch.

If a licence is desired, similar formalities must be observed as when procuring one for use in a church, and one day must elapse between its issue and the wedding.

No minister of religion need be present at a civil contract, even if it take place in a chapel or building certified for marriages. Members of the Society of Friends may, after giving notice as above described, be married in their Meeting House; but to make it legal, the fact must be duly registered {84} by the officer of the district as soon after the ceremony as possible.

The presence of a registrar is not necessary at marriages performed in Nonconformist chapels if they are duly certified and an "authorised person" (that is, one duly appointed by the trustees or governing body of the building) is present during the proceedings. Certain declarations, similar to those made before the registrar, must be included in any form of service. The "authorised person" must register the marriage at his earliest convenience.

Fees for Civil Contract.

A marriage by certificate costs about ten or twelve shillings. With a licence, the expense mounts up to about £2, 15s.

Settlements.

This is a matter of cold unromantic fact, and one which very ardent, impossible lovers regard almost in the light of a desecration. As the prosaic side of life has to be faced, it is very necessary that money matters should find a place in the matrimonial preparations.

An honourable man is always anxious to effect some arrangement by which his wife may be safeguarded from ruin or extreme poverty. If she has money of her own, he will see that it is settled upon her absolutely. Should he raise, or even hint at, an objection to this plan, he will lay himself open to a serious charge of possessing mercenary motives. A man with private means would settle a certain portion upon his wife; but, in the ordinary course of things, she would only have the interest of this amount, and would not have control over the capital during his life. At the same time, it could not be touched by his creditors.

In more legal language: "By marriage settlements the property to be settled by one or both of the parties is conveyed to trustees upon trust as to the lady's property for her separate use during her life, and after her decease for the husband for his life. The husband's property is settled on him for life with remainder to the wife for life. On the death of the survivor the trust is for the children of the marriage in such {85} shares as the husband and wife, or the survivor, appoint, and in default of appointment among the children equally." Clauses as to maintenance and education of the children, and powers of investment of trust funds, are inserted. In settling large estates and sums of money various modes of settlement are adopted to suit the circumstances, but the above is the outline of an ordinary settlement. Large landed estates are generally settled, after the decease of the settlers, upon the first and other sons in tail male with cross remainders between them, and in default of male issue among the daughters.

The Bride's Dowry,

or marriage portion, is of very ancient origin. Even two centuries before Christ the wealth possessed by a woman brought her an increase of respect from her husband, and lessened the humiliation of her legal and social position. By degrees the rich wife gained the upper hand, and what the law would not give to her sex as a right, she obtained by virtue of her money.

CHAPTER XV

The Wedding-Day--What is expected of (1) The Bride; (2) The Bridesmaids; (3) The Bridegroom; (4) The Best Man; (5) The Bride's Parents--At the Bride's House--Dressing--Starting for the Church--The Tying of the Knot--Social Aspect--Reception or Breakfast.

The Wedding-Day.

"Happy is the Bride that the Sun shines on!" runs the old adage, but we may hope that the lives of all English brides are not as grey as the skies under which they are often married. We can also hope that every bride will have the sunshine of joy in her heart on her wedding-day. Most weddings now take place at 2 o'clock or 2.30, in consequence of the extension of the marriage hours, and this has in a great measure abolished the old "breakfast," which was a rather trying affair for all concerned. Now, a more informal reception takes place on the return from church, with champagne, tea, ices, and all sorts of pretty light refreshments. Those who, from choice or force of circumstances, decide upon the morning for the ceremony, would naturally give a luncheon, but the smarter section of society has spoken in favour of the reception.

I know of a capricious couple who played their friends a very shabby trick. The invitations had been issued for a Wednesday, and at the last moment they decided to be married on the Tuesday morning. They went quietly to church in the early hours, left the town separately during the day, met in London, and started for the honeymoon. The next afternoon their friends assembled to find that the objects of their congratulations were away across the Channel. This was a most serious breach of etiquette, as there was no reason for such rudeness.

What is Expected of the Bride.

However long and frequent the visits of the *fiancé* have been to his sweetheart's home, tradition decrees that he must not sleep under the same roof with her the night before the wedding, nor is he supposed to see her on the day, till he meets her in all her bridal beauty. She is supposed to keep in retirement even from the members of her own household during the early part of the day; but this is a matter of opinion, and all old ideas are giving way to more modern views.

On her wedding-day, at least if it is to be a smart affair, the bride is handicapped as well as adorned by her clothes, as seems to be the general lot of women on all important occasions. Let us hope that every care has been taken to minimise the minor anxieties as to the fit of her frock, the set of her veil, the comfort of shoes and gloves. She must feel something like a *débutante* dressing for her presentation at court; but while the latter is only making her entry into society, the bride is entering upon a condition that will affect her eternally, and one that ought to have the blessing of God upon it. One would therefore like the bride to be free from such inconveniences as will drag her down mentally. Let her be free to respond to the high inspirations and holy desires that best become a woman on this great day of her life. She will probably be nervous, and small wonder, but she will be none the less attractive for a little maidenly diffidence. The bride who marches triumphantly through her wedding does not show the best taste. In the rush and excitement of the wedding morning some one must make a point of seeing that the bride has proper food to sustain her through her part in the day's proceedings. Her appearance will not be improved by the look of strained weariness that combined fatigue and exhaustion will bring even into the youngest face. She is expected to look her best and to have her emotions under control nowadays. The weeping bride is out of date. She is expected to look happy, for is she not completing the choice which she freely made? If her shoes pinch, or she is faint from hunger, those expectations cannot be fulfilled.

The Bridesmaids.

These attendant maidens must be at the church awaiting the bride, ready to follow her up the aisle, and the chief one {88} takes her place so as to be prepared to receive the gloves and bouquet from the bride before the putting on of the ring. One or more of them will help the bride, later in the day, to change into her travelling costume, and they can be of assistance in countless ways, both to the hostess and her guests. Sometimes, however, a bridesmaid is too occupied preparing for another wedding, in which she will play the chief part, to have much time for any one else.

The Bridegroom.

Though of the highest and most vital importance, the bridegroom never seems quite so much to the fore as the bride. It is probably a mere matter of clothes. He is expected to have the ring in readiness, to provide a conveyance to take himself and the best man to the scene of the ceremony, and, above all, to be in good time, waiting in proud anticipation for the bride's arrival. He does not always look happy or quite at his ease with the eyes of the curious congregation upon him, but that is only his modesty. He has to give the bridesmaids a present (generally some trinket is chosen), and the bride receives her bouquet from him. Sometimes the best man gives the bridesmaids their bouquets, but it is generally the bridegroom, unless they are all related together.

The Best Man.

I have heard it said that the office of the Best Man is to see that the bridegroom does not run away at the last moment. We will hope he does not often have hard work in that case. He certainly has to see that love does not make the bridegroom oblivious to the practical details of life. He escorts him to church and supports him through the service. He pays the fees of clerk and clergyman and calls the carriages when the register is signed. He is a very busy and useful person, if he does his duty, and much of the success from a social point of view may lie in his hands.

The Bride's Parents.

The heaviest burden of responsibility falls upon the shoulders of the bride's mother. She has to arrange with a caterer for the refreshments, unless she prefers to have all the trouble of {89} preparing them at home; she must order the carriages, arrange the meals for guests staying in the house, and settle the order in which the wedding party is to go to church. She has to see about floral decorations wherever they are wanted, and now flowers play such an all-important part in every festivity. She will be the one to whom every one will go for instructions, and it may be her own heart will be very sore at the thought of parting with her daughter. Where there are other grown-up girls they would naturally take some portion of the work off her hands, but she is nominal head of affairs in most households.

The *father* has to escort his daughter to church and bestow her upon her husband. In the event of his being prevented from doing this, her mother would drive with her, and the relation or friend who was acting as her father's deputy would meet her at the church door. The bride's father pays all the expenses of music or decoration in the church in addition to those of entertainment at home and conveyances. He will find the bill a large one in these days of lavish display and increased luxury. The idea that a reception is much cheaper than a luncheon is balanced by the facts that a far larger number of people can be included in the former and that champagne cannot be dispensed with.

At the Bride's House.

Before the appointed hour, bustle and possible confusion will reign in the bride's home. The young people will take a pride in decking the reception-rooms with flowers. The presents will be in a room by themselves, and will probably have been arranged the day before, but there are always a hundred little finishing touches to be put to everything. The caterer will, if required, supply all needful glass, china, tables, and attendance for the reception or breakfast. Everyone should be dressed in good time. There will be belated presents, telegrams of congratulation, and all sorts of minor distractions.

Dressing the Bride.

In many cases the dressmaker who has *created* the wedding gown comes to see it put on, but where such skilled help is not required the loving hands of mother, sister, or friend would deck the bride. One thing I would suggest. It is a risk {90} to dress the hair to suit the veil rather than the face. I remember seeing a bride quite spoiled by having her pretty hair dragged up under her veil, when as a rule she wore it in soft, natural waves round her face and ears. The less jewellery a bride wears the better, and some recent leaders of fashion have exchanged the bridal bouquet for a prayer-book, which they carried in ungloved hands. A bride who is married in the veil of a happy wife is supposed to be lucky. It is a pretty idea for a girl to wear her mother's bridal veil.

The Tying of the Knot.

When she is ready and all the others have started for the church, the bride drives with her father or mother, as the case may be, away from her old home and her maiden name. These few moments are too sacred for an outsider to speak of. Upon her arrival the bells ring out, the choir and clergy form the head of the procession, and she goes up to the chancel step on her father's right arm to take her place on the left side of her expectant bridegroom. It seems almost an impertinence to tell her how she should look at this solemn time, but it is not necessary or seemly for her to smile and nod to her friends in the church. She should remove both gloves on taking her place, so that she may be prepared to take the bridegroom by the hand and to receive the ring.

Arrangement of Seats.

The brothers or cousins of the bride show the guests to their seats in church. The bridegroom's family and friends sit on the right as they enter, the bride's party on the left. Parents and nearest relations occupy the front seats, then others in order of kinship.

As soon as the service is over, the newly-wedded pair, and such of their relations and friends as have been asked to do so, withdraw to the vestry, where the register is duly signed and witnessed.

The Social Side.

The bride and bridegroom drive off first from the church, so as to be in readiness to receive the congratulations of the {91} guests, who greet them immediately upon returning to the house. They are the principal people for the time being. The parents follow in the next carriage, her father taking his mother. Where there are many guests, no one should expect to take up much of the bride's attention, as she will have to divide her favours among the company. If there is a sit-down meal, she would be between her husband and father. The newly-married pair would either take the head of the table or sit in the centre of one side of the festive board. The practice of making long speeches has fallen into disuse, and every bride must be thankful for the relief. At an informal reception, where there is a chance to move about, the strain is not so great; but whichever form of entertainment is chosen, the bride *must cut the cake*, and every one is invited to partake of it.

Some Items of Expense.

The supply of carriages should be sufficient to enable all the guests to be conveyed to and from the church with as little delay as possible, and each carriage and pair will cost from 12s. 6d. to 15s., while a guinea is charged for the bride's special equipage. Grey horses are extra, but few people have them now, as it gives the situation away. Each driver will expect a tip of a few shillings.

A simple 5lb. wedding-cake can be had for 8s. or 10s., but the larger and more elaborate ones run up to £5 and £8, the ornamental stands being extra. Of course there is practically no limit to expenses if people wish to throw money about. One American wedding cost over a million dollars. At another the wedding-cake was stuffed with expensive gewgaws, and as it weighed a quarter of a ton it was conveyed on silver tram lines up and down the table or buffet.

The bouquets for the bridesmaids cost anything from 15s. to £5, while that for the bride may run from £4 to £10, or as much more as the bridegroom likes to give.

Many people who do not want their homes turned upside down or whose houses are not convenient for a wedding, entertain their friends at an hotel or a restaurant. This has its advantages, but is not so homelike for the bride's farewell to her old associations and home life.

CHAPTER XVI

The Guests--The Presents on View--Starting for the Honeymoon--Dress and Luggage--Where to Go and How Long to Stay--Inevitable Test of Temperament--Possible Disappointments--Disillusion, Passing or Permanent.

The Guests.

The average crowd, mainly composed of women, who throng to see a wedding are unfortunately notorious for their utter lack of reverence and total want of manners. The invited guests do not always behave in accordance with the rules of etiquette. One hears a running fire of comments, such as: "They say she's marrying him for his money!" or "Well, her mother ought to be glad; she's worked hard enough to catch him." "He's stepping into a nice thing. I suppose the old boy paid his debts!"

Frequent allusions to former flirtations, or worse, are made in a stage whisper, and open expression is given to the question: "How long will it last?" by the cynics who seem to have come to be disagreeable. A wedding is bound to call forth both retrospective and anticipatory thoughts, but all unkind words should be silenced by a common desire to let that one day pass happily for all. Guests who snatch at wedding-favours to take home, who are boisterous in their leave-taking of the departing couple, who stay to the bitter end and pocket morsels of bridecake, who loudly appraise the value of the presents, or audibly speculate as to "what it has cost So-and-So to get his daughter off," have as yet to learn the rudiments of etiquette.

{93}

The Presents on View.

The hostess should see that all the guests have opportunities of seeing the wedding presents; but it is not judicious for visitors at a big function to poke about among the gifts unless accompanied by one of the family or, perhaps, a bridesmaid, because it is generally deemed wise to have a detective present on such an occasion, and he might misinterpret this friendly interest to the discomfort of the prying guests. In arranging the presents a nice thoughtfulness and tact are necessary. Let the smaller offerings have due prominence, for the sake of the kindly thought that prompted them. One who had not been able to afford a gift in any proportion to her affection would feel touched by its occupying a place of honour.

Starting for the Honeymoon.

As the time for departure draws near the bride will slip away to doff her bridal splendour for her travelling costume. Her sister, the favourite bridesmaid, or her mother will doubtless go and help her, and probably some of the real "Good-byes" will be spoken before she rejoins the company. The dress will have been chosen with reference to the journey she is now undertaking. If she has but a short distance to go it may be a picturesque, dainty creation, but if she has hard travelling before her it will be of the tailor-made type, at once stylish and business-like, devoid of unnecessary fallals.

All present will be anxious to take leave of the newly-wedded pair, and to wish them God-speed. There is often deep sorrow under the surface of merriment at such partings. It is the moment when young brothers and frivolous cousins perform impish pranks, while the parents, and maybe the bride, are feeling the keen pang of separation. Paper confetti are a harmless substitute for rice, which is not soothing to receive in the eye or ear. The throwing of old shoes is said to be a relic of the sticks and stones hurled in wrath by the defeated friends of the bride when the victorious bridegroom carried her off as his prize and captive.

The Journey.

Many are the devices resorted to by the newly married to escape detection on the wedding journey. Some take old battered portmanteaux. I have heard of a baby being borrowed to block up the window of the railway carriage; but matrimony, like murder, will out. The bridegroom will naturally do all in his power to make the journey an ideally pleasant one, and he will do well to remember that his bride has had much more to strain her nerves and weary her than he has.

Luggage.

At any time it seems well to avoid a number of small parcels, but on this occasion it is doubly advisable. Even if the husband and wife can fix their minds on such prosaic things, it is hardly fair for her to hang him round with her bags, hat-boxes, and other feminine impedimenta. On the other hand, if he has brought his cycle, his golf clubs, his fishing-tackle, and his camera, his attention is bound to be divided between the safety of his possessions and the comfort of his bride.

Where to Go.

The destination of the honeymooners will depend upon the time they have to spare, the money they can spend, and their combined tastes. There are a few practical hints that may be given. It is often said that travelling is one of the best tests of temper, so let the woman who soon feels fretted and looks jaded or is physically indisposed by a long railway journey take her honeymoon near home. Let no one who is not reliably happy on board ship attempt to cross the water and run the risk of ending her wedding-day in the terribly unbecoming condition caused by *mal de mer*.

How Long to Stay.

The modern tendency to shorten honeymoons seems born of wisdom as much as of expediency. It may sound brutal, but undisturbed possession soon palls, and man was made {95} for something more virile than perpetual billing and cooing. The long honeymoon makes a very heavy demand upon the emotions. It is fatal to try and keep up a lost illusion. The moment a man or woman sees that the sweetness is beginning to cloy, and the inaction to bore, it is time to return to everyday life.

Inevitable Test of Temperament.

The honeymoon is bound to disclose many hitherto unsuspected phases of character. These revelations will be in proportion to the amount of previous mutual understanding. The lover who has been free-handed may turn into the husband who haggles over his hotel bills. The girl who has always looked like a dainty picture (because there was some one to take care of her things) may be careless and unkempt when there is no one but her husband to see her. The man who had preferred a sandwich in the woods with his beloved, may be the one to swear at the waiter if the made dishes are not exactly to his taste. The sweetheart who has been all smiles, may prove but a sorry companion when exposed to discomfort, and show herself quite unable to rise cheerfully to an emergency.

On the other hand, surprises of a pleasant nature may be in store for bride and bridegroom. Unthought of qualities may be called into play, deeper feelings may be aroused, and the full sweetness of a character only be fully revealed in the sacred privacy of the honeymoon.

Possible Disappointments.

A modern writer says: "How many ideals are shattered by the intimacy of marriage, simply because the antenuptial love has been based upon fiction and misunderstanding. If only a man and a woman made their several motives for marrying quite clear to one another, and were not quite so anxious to preserve a veneer of romance up to the very altar, matrimony would not be the terrible iconoclast it too often is." This is plain speaking, and one wonders how many marriages would ever take place if this precept were carried out. It is true that much has to be revealed after marriage. The {96} lover has only seen his sweetheart when she has placed herself on view, so to speak. They were both kept in check by the uncertainty of their position. The husband sees his wife under all circumstances, in mentally trying moments, in physically unbecoming situations. In fact, she has to appear before him with her hair out of curl, actually and metaphorically, to use a homely illustration.

Disillusion, Passing or Permanent.

The mental relations between husband and wife must necessarily differ from those between lovers, and the more honest and sincere they have been during their courtship, the less painful will be the awakening after marriage. Where there is both love and trust, coupled with common sense, a little humour, and a broad view of life, the disillusion should only be a passing cloud that makes the sunshine all the brighter for its temporary shade. Where there has been conscious, or even involuntary, deception, an unreal position or exaggerated idealisation on either side, the pain of disillusion will be poignant, and its effect permanent. Things can be sorrowfully and bravely patched up for mere outward use, but there will be a smart under the smile, and a blank in the life that should have been so full.

Whatever mental crisis may follow marriage, the two who suffer, for one seldom suffers alone, will do well to keep their own counsel. If the silence is too great a strain, it is wiser, though perhaps not so natural, to seek help from some trusted friend unconnected by kinship with either family. Relations cannot take an unprejudiced view of the case; they are bound to be biassed in favour of their own, and even if family jars are not openly discussed the leaven works, and its effect is soon perceptible.

{97}

CHAPTER XVII

The Return Home--A Plunge into the Practical--Housekeeping--Wedding Calls--The Newly-married Couple at Home and in Society.

The Return Home.

It is the unanimous and unqualified opinion of those who know, that the first year of married life practically answers the question "Is Marriage a Failure?" The bride who can emerge triumphantly from this searching ordeal will hold her own for the rest of her career as a wife. The newly-married girl or woman has everything to try her mettle. The end of the honeymoon sees the beginning of her real work. She has won her husband; she has charmed and satisfied him in the hours of love in idleness; she has now to keep him true to his allegiance through the dull prosaic days of ordinary, humdrum life. For the husband the change is not nearly so great. He has his usual daily avocations to follow; his business or professional duties have undergone no alteration.

We will hope the wedded pair have a nice cosy home awaiting their return. If the honeymoon has been short, the bulk of the preparations will have been made before the wedding, and a mother or sister will have put the finishing touches during the bride's absence, but no one should be awaiting them in their new home except the servants they have engaged. It may be that there is a visit to be paid to relations before settling into the new home, and this will be a little trying. Those who love them and who watch them start on their wedding journey will eagerly scan their features for some sign to indicate how things have gone with them in this important interval. A happy heart need shun {98} no such scrutiny, but where the slightest wound is hidden under smiles the loving solicitude will give pain.

A Plunge into the Practical.

Whatever the nature of the new home may be, whether mansion or cottage, town flat or suburban villa, even if it be but the temporary resting-place of furnished rooms, the wife will do well to begin by studying her husband's comfort, and finding out any special likes and dislikes that may not as yet have come under her notice. He, for his part, must not expect too much, and should try not to make her painfully conscious of her shortcomings. He might also reflect with advantage, when things are not to his taste, that he has himself to thank for a good deal. He chose his wife for her youth, her beauty, her charm, or her money it may be, and he then asked for no other qualification. He took up all her thoughts and her spare time during their engagement, and all he asked was that she should look nice and let him make love to her. She was purely ornamental in those days, and he was content to have her so. Once marriage is over he expects her to develop exactly those domestic gifts that shall best minister to his comfort and well-being. This cannot be done in a day.

Housekeeping.

Apart from the strangeness of her position, her probable isolation from all familiar faces, her mingled sense of freedom and responsibility, the young wife has much to contend with. Housekeeping comes more easily to some women than to others, and the one who has a domestic gift scores a big point in starting married life. The girl who has had no previous training or practical experience will spend many a bitter moment face to face with her own utter incompetence. The servant question alone is enough for most people. The young maid knows her new mistress is but a novice; the experienced cook regards her either from a motherly point of view or in the light of lawful prey. She has, however, to maintain her dignity in the face of all this. She knows her ignorance will be detected and possibly laughed at, behind her back, but she {99} must not compromise the position in which her husband has placed her by undue familiarity, or undignified relations with those over whom she is to preside. By this it is not meant that a mistress should be afraid of being civil and even friendly with her maids;

but she must discern nicely between that which breeds contempt and that which adds affection to respect.

Money Matters.

Many girls have had no money to manage beyond the spending of a dress allowance, with an indulgent parent always ready to make up the deficit. It would be well for every mother to give the housekeeping accounts into the hands of her engaged daughter for at least a month before she marries. She will not master the subject, but she will acquire some idea of the just prices of household commodities, and the quantities that should be ordered. The bride who suggested the leg of beef "for a change" is happily fictional, but it is to be feared that many do not much exceed her in knowledge. Some men give their wives a regular weekly allowance for domestic expenses, and this seems a fair way to do things. Others believe in paying everything by cheque, and thus keep all the money in their own hands. Provided the husband is pleasant when the cheques are drawn out the wife is saved a great deal of trouble; but the man who swears over the monthly bill, and wants an account of every pound of meat consumed in that time, creates a perpetual burden for his luckless partner. The early mismanagement of household expenses is fraught with sorrow to the well-meaning wife and heart-searchings to the husband, who begins to ask anxiously: "Could I really afford to marry?" Whatever the precise nature of the arrangement may be, there should be a clear understanding as to how the expenses are to be divided. Supposing the wife has her own income, or an allowance from her husband, she ought to know exactly what that sum is expected to cover. She is also entitled to a definite knowledge as to the extent of his income. Many a tragedy might have been averted if the wife had been taken earlier into the husband's confidence.

Wedding Calls.

There is much diversity of opinion as to how the bride is to make her home-coming known to her friends. The fashion of sending wedding-cards is pronounced out of date, and they are only now tolerated when enclosed with wedding-cake to old friends. It is no longer necessary for the bride to sit at home in expectant and solitary grandeur, waiting for the callers to make their appearance. She is free to go out and about as she pleases, unless, of course, she has fixed any date upon which to receive friends. She must be careful to return all the calls made upon her in due time, and should note the At Home days and addresses of her new acquaintances. The simplest way is to let the date of return filter out through friends, and if any one is really anxious to call she will find out when to do so. In the suburbs and in country towns the bride may quite well give an At Home to the friends who gave her presents, and to those who were at her wedding, without waiting for them to call upon her. The invitations would be sent out in the wife's name only, but her husband would put in an appearance if possible. The bride would receive her friends in one of her dainty new frocks, and though there would be no formal display of presents, those who had given her pretty things would be pleased to see them put to their appointed uses. It is not a bride's place to start an acquaintance with older married people, nor is she expected to entertain upon a large scale during the early part of her married life. In certain cases, notably those of professional men, the social success of the young wife may materially affect the financial position of her husband. I knew of a doctor's bride who gave great offence to his patients by omitting to return her wedding calls until after her first child was born.

The Newly-married Couple at Home.

Loneliness is one of the bride's trials. She is alone the greater part of the day. Her things are all new, and do not require much attention in the way of mending or altering. Her household is but small, and once she has had her morning interview with the cook there is not much for her to do. The novelty of her position makes her restless, and averse to {101} going on with the pursuits that have been interrupted by her marriage. The old familiar home life is exchanged for solitary sway, and she does not always know how to fill up the long hours. She gets nervous, over-wrought, and is sometimes driven out of her new home in search of excitement.

The woman who marries on a small income and has plenty of work to do is not so liable to this unfortunate development.

The husband should be prepared for the effect of this uprooting on his young wife. He must not grudge her the little diversions that will help to pass the time while he is away. A woman with tact will choose the right moment for unburdening her mind of domestic woes. It is generally considered a wise plan to give a man a good dinner before you tell him anything unpleasant. The less she tells him of her petty worries the better a wife will get on, and the more her husband will admire her. Real troubles and grave anxieties should always be shared, and both authority and responsibility should be divided in a household if things are to run smoothly. It will be well for the young wife if she can feel the matrimonial ground firmly beneath her feet before she is called upon to bear the additional anxieties and physical trials of approaching motherhood.

In Society.

The bride is the honoured guest at any party given on her account. She would naturally appear in white, and if it were a grand affair she might don a modified edition of the wedding gown. I know a youthful bride who, having been married in a travelling dress, ordered a white satin frock at her husband's expense in which to make her social *début*. The average newly-married couple are not the most entertaining companions. Their own little world is too absorbing for them to take much interest in the trifles outside it, but it is beautiful to see their happiness. Sometimes they are tiresome. The bride is the chief offender. She quotes her Adolphus as the world-oracle, and dilates on her own recent domestic discoveries as if they were what civilised humanity had been waiting for through dark ages of perplexity. Her superior attitude towards unmarried friends not unfrequently leads to friction.

We must have patience with her, for she is learning a great deal, and has not yet had time to sort it out into proper proportions.

CHAPTER XVIII

Mixed Marriages--Differences of Colour--Nationality and Religion--Scotch Marriages--Marriage of Minors and Wards in Chancery.

Mixed Marriages.

Love overleaps all barriers, and it is of but little use to try and bind it. Marriage, however, is another thing, and can be prevented even where love exists. How far it is right or advisable to do so must be a matter of individual judgment decided by the facts of each separate case. To take an instance. There is a very strong feeling, especially among medical men, against the marriage of cousins. Now love deep and true may exist between two cousins; but, seeing the physical deterioration that comes from the intermarrying of members of one family, it may be a plain duty to unborn generations for these two to abstain from marriage with each other. Where there is any hereditary disease of mind or body it is little short of criminal to contract such a union. In the matter of *Mixed Marriages*--namely, those between men and women differing from each other in colour, nationality, or religion, it is generally thought that they are fraught with grave risks.

The Question of Colour.

This does not affect us here in England as much as it does in India and those parts of the empire where there is a coloured native population. To those who have lived among {103} it the question is one of burning importance. We cannot go into it here, but, seeing that these marriages do take place even in England, a word of warning may not be amiss. Women who are fascinated by coloured men would do well to note that there is not a white man, good, bad, or indifferent, who does not abhor the idea of a white woman's marrying a coloured man. This is not the outcome of jealousy, nor yet of ignorance, for the more the European has travelled the more rooted is his aversion to such unions. He knows, as man with man, what the real mental attitude of those dusky gentlemen is towards women. He knows what lies behind the courtly manner, the nameless grace, and sensuous charm of these impassioned lovers. No woman can know this till after marriage, and then the knowledge does not do her much good. Let any woman who contemplates a marriage with a coloured man, no matter how high his caste may be, take counsel with some man who has lived among the dark races and who cannot possibly be suspected of jealousy, and she will learn that which may save her from an infinity of suffering.

Different Nationalities.

Among Europeans intermarriage is fairly frequent, and may turn out well. No doubt it is a success in many cases, but where it is, I think it will be found that either the man has become cosmopolitan in his ideas or the woman has lived long enough abroad to fit in with continental modes of life. The English girl who has been educated in a French convent will not have the same difficulty in pleasing a French husband or adapting herself to his ways as the home-reared girl who meets "Monsieur Blanc" on her first visit to the Continent.

Without a fairly wide knowledge of the home life to which marriage with a foreigner will lead, an English, Scotch, or Irish girl is running a great risk by taking such a final step as matrimony, for in no other country in Europe have women quite the same position as in the British Isles. The more restricted the mental horizon of the one may be, the less likelihood is there of perfect sympathy between husband and wife.

The Necessary Formalities.

Where such a marriage has been decided upon, there are many preliminary regulations to be observed. As my legal friend remarks: "A strict observance of the marriage laws of foreign countries, where one of the parties to a marriage is English and it takes place in England, is most necessary, or a person may find herself or himself married in England but legally repudiated abroad. In France the consent of parents is required up to the age of twenty-five, and if refused, what are called three respectful summonses are to be made. If consent be still withheld, the party can marry legally." There was a case recently in the English papers of a marriage between two French people being annulled because the ceremony had been performed in England without the proper formalities having been observed in France.

"In Germany the fact of the betrothal and intention to marry must be advertised in newspapers circulating in the district or districts in which the parties reside, and if one of them resides in England then in an English newspaper. In Germany notice has also to be given to the town-clerk or some like official."

Any marriage that is legal in the country where it is contracted is valid in Switzerland. An Englishwoman marrying an Italian may be married in England according to the rites of her own church, but a copy of the marriage certificate must be sent to the nearest Italian consul, who forwards it to the authorities of the man's native town or place of residence. There should be no delay in doing this, as no marriage is legal in Italy if not registered within three months of its celebration.

There have been so many sad results from irregular mixed marriages that at the February meeting of the Lower House of Convocation at York a resolution was moved: "In view of the grave scandals arising in respect to marriages between English and foreign subjects asking the Upper House to consider the desirability of issuing an order to the beneficed clergy and the diocesan registrars requiring that when a foreigner gives notice of his intention to be married to an English subject the marriage should not be solemnised till a consular certificate was produced that the laws of the foreign country had been complied with."

British Subjects Living Abroad.

No British subject, especially a woman, should agree to any form of marriage without having first applied to the British consul of the district, or to the embassy if there is one, for full particulars and instructions for the contracting of a legal marriage in a foreign country under the *Foreign Marriage Act of* 1892. An Englishwoman takes the nationality of the man she marries.

A marriage that would be illegal in England is unaffected by any ceremony performed in the presence of authorised persons abroad should the parties return to this country. For instance, a man who wishes to marry his deceased wife's sister can go to a country where such a marriage is legal and be married; but if the couple return to England they are not man and wife in the eyes of the law.

Different Religious Persuasions.

Where there is a difference of religious faith and practice between the man and woman, there will not only be the marriage ceremony to arrange but there should be a clear, written agreement as to which faith any children that may be born are to be reared in. The Roman Church does not recognise marriage except when solemnised by her own priests, but if one of the parties is not a Romanist the ceremony may be afterwards gone through in an English church or Nonconformist chapel. A Jew in England can be married by a registrar, but probably the majority of Jews in England are married in a synagogue, in which case a registrar is in attendance.

Any one who marries a Romanist should bear in mind that the dearest aim of every faithful member of their Church is to bring others into the fold. Many Nonconformists are willing and even anxious to be married in the parish church of their district. It may be generally said, save in the above-named case, that the woman gets her own way about the religious ceremony. Where strong prejudice exists on either side the matter may be settled by a civil contract; but apart from the real question of religion, marriage before a registrar has not the {106} social prestige which still clings to the time-honoured custom of exchanging marital vows in the House of God.

Scotch Marriages.

The old law as to Scotch irregular marriages has been modified of late years, and Gretna marriages are no longer recognised.

Twenty-one days' residence since 1896 is required, but otherwise acknowledgment before witnesses is a legal marriage. In the year 1878 an Act entitled *An Act to encourage Regular Marriage in Scotland* was passed, and under it ministers may celebrate marriages on a certificate from a registrar, which is equivalent to the publication of banns. This certificate is issued by registrars on receiving notice of the intended marriage. The registrar posts the notice in the prescribed mode, and, if no objection is received, grants his certificate. The notice must be given to the registrar of the district or districts in which the parties have resided for fifteen days at least.

Marriage of Minors and Wards in Chancery.

If a minor who is a ward in Chancery marries without the consent of the Lord Chancellor (who takes care that proper settlements are made of the ward's property), he or she commits a contempt of court, and is liable to punishment accordingly. A minor who will inherit property can be made a ward by settling £100 upon him or her and making a proper application to the court. There is no law against two minors marrying, but the consent of parents is required.

{107}

CHAPTER XIX

Foreign Etiquette of Marriage--Quaint Customs and Strange Superstitions.

Continental Weddings.

Many of the national, picturesque customs have disappeared from the weddings of the townspeople and the more educated classes on the Continent; but many distinctive points of etiquette still remain, and we shall find that in matters of detail there is much that differs from our English ways.

In *Germany* it is impossible for young people to marry without the consent of their parents or legal guardians, and unless certain prescribed forms are gone through, the marriage will be null and void. So many certificates of birth, parentage, etc., have to be produced that, it is said, the working classes can neither afford the time nor the money necessary for a legal marriage; so many of them do without it. The husband is the lord and master; his wife's property passes into his keeping and is at his absolute disposal. He may compel her to work, and even if the pair be divorced he still retains her money. As German girls are brought up to expect this, it does not strike them as any hardship, and most of them are quite happy to be under the sway of their liege lords.

The chief festivity of a German wedding is the *Polterabend*, a somewhat hilarious party given the night before. The young friends of the bride enact charades, or give living pictures illustrative of the chief events in her childhood and youth. There is much merriment, and, I believe, the breaking of crockery has a part in the proceedings. The bridesmaids are accompanied by an equal number of young men, called *Brautführer*. The bridal wreath is always of myrtle, not orange blossom, and the bride and bridegroom exchange rings. Customs vary according to social station and locality.

{108} At a South German peasant's wedding there is wild rejoicing and much ceremony. The guests are invited by a messenger, who draws devices on the doorsteps of those he has to summon to the feast. There is music and dancing, processions are formed to and from the church, the bride is hailed with flowers, and all sorts of emblematical offerings are taken to church. The bridegroom stuffs his pockets with samples of what he hopes will constitute his worldly wealth. If he never looks back between the house and the altar, the bride knows that he will never want a second wife. For those who have the leisure and opportunity to study these peasant marriages a curious compound of sentiment, superstition, and practical common sense will present itself.

In Norway

the bride who has preserved her maiden state untarnished--it is not necessarily expected of her--is crowned with a high, glittering crown inlaid with gems, which is the property of the church, and can be hired for five dollars. Special music is also performed in her honour by the rustic musicians. Wedding festivities are marked by unbounded hospitality. There is food and drink for all. When the procession is formed the bride walks last, clad in a gorgeous costume which also may be hired. There are both bridesmaids and bride-leaders, the latter being married women who lend their moral support to the bride. The couple kneel in the church under a sort of canopy made out of shawls and scarves held up by the bridesmaids. After the ceremony an amount of eating, drinking, and dancing go on that we can hardly imagine. The bridegroom has a last sort of romp with his bachelor friends, and has to be wrested from them by the married men. The bride dances off her crown, is then blindfolded and surrounded by a ring of her bridesmaids, and places her crown upon the head of one of them who is claimed as the next bride. Before the cake is cut each friend lays a coin upon it, and toasts are drunk with enthusiasm. In some provinces the bride has to run away and hide the day after the wedding. A grand search is then made, and she is carried home with much ado. This practice still prevails among some of the native African tribes and the aborigines of Australia.

In Brittany

the bridegroom pretends to "capture" his bride. He makes a mock assault upon her house, which is carefully closed with locks and bolts against him. The besieging party take bagpipes to while away the time. Much parleying goes on, and every female member of the bride's family is offered to the bridegroom by one of her male relations, who is the chosen tormentor. When she finally does appear the pair exchange sprigs of myrtle or orange blossom, and there is a dance. Before the party starts for the church they all kneel in prayer, and the bride takes a touching farewell of her parents. Feasting and revelry finish up the day.

In Italy

the bride becomes entirely one of her husband's family, and his mother is all-powerful. Before the marriage the couple, accompanied by three witnesses, must go before the appointed authorities, and a document is drawn up stating that they wish to marry. The witnesses sign this paper to show that there is no impediment to the marriage. The document is then posted up outside a stated public building for the inspection of the passers-by. If no one makes any objection before the end of a fortnight, the couple may then make a legal civil contract, and nothing more is required. This arrangement was made to check the power of the priests, who manipulated marriages much to their own fancy under the Papal government. A youth must be eighteen and a girl sixteen before they can marry. There are many superstitions about the lucky and unlucky days for marriages. Sunday is the favoured day. There are hardly ever any bridesmaids at an Italian wedding, as girls are not supposed to be present on such occasions, so the married women accompany the bride.

In Russia

no man under thirty nor woman under twenty-five may marry without the consent of parents, but in the event of unreasonable opposition an appeal may be made to the law. Both bride and bridegroom must give costly presents {110} to the Church. The man comes to claim his bride from her parents, and she kneels before them to ask pardon for all she may have done to vex or grieve them. They raise her with a kiss of forgiveness, and give her bread and salt in token that they will never let her want. When she leaves her old home the door is left open as a sign that she may always return to it. Rich brides wear nothing but white and orange blossom; but pale blue and a coronet of silver ribbon are more in accordance with the national custom. The religious ceremony has all the ritual and grandeur of the Greek Church. The bride has to prostrate herself before her husband in token of entire submission. The best man attends the bride, not the bridegroom, and is chosen by her. Seven o'clock in the evening is the time for Russian weddings to begin. Mostly newly-married couples live with the husband's family, who greet them on their return from church with bread and salt. A dance follows, during which the bride has to change her dress as many times as she has different costumes in her trousseau. The supper is served at daybreak, after which the guests depart. In Russia the wife's name is always a little different from that of her husband, owing to the fact that the family name when borne by a male is a substantive and can be used alone, while in a lady's case it is only an adjective which requires completion to give it full meaning.

In Sweden

a rainy day is considered lucky for a marriage, as it foretells wealth. There is barbaric feasting at the wedding, and departing guests are given a bottle of brandy and a huge ring of wheaten bread with which to treat those they meet on their way home. The bride is dressed by her particular friend, or by the pastor's wife, and wears a black, beribboned gown, ornamented with mock gems, tinsel, and artificial flowers. She has a myrtle wreath or a crown like her Norwegian sister. Her shoes have some symbolical reference to possible motherhood. In the left one her father places a silver coin, while her mother puts gold in the right shoe. These represent the necessaries and luxuries with which they hope she will be provided. On her return from church her mother places a sweetmeat in her mouth to make her gentle of speech.

{111}

In Spain

the bride always retains her maiden name attached to that of her husband, and both must be used together. Flowers form a great feature of Spanish marriages, and in each district blossoms have special significance. In Valentia the ceremony takes place at night, and there is a mock "marriage by capture." All the guests must leave by 1 A.M. In Catalonia only the nearest relations of the pair are allowed to attend the service, but many guests are asked to the house, and each must bring a gift. It is an insult to refuse an invitation of this kind. The guests are divided according to sex, and when the bridegroom is tired of the men he goes and throws sweets at the ladies, exclusive of his wife. Then dancing follows. The bride's father gives his daughter her house, furniture, and trousseau, while the guests are supposed to supply her dowry. In Andalusia no ring is used, but every married woman wears flowers in her hair over the right ear as a mark of her matronly dignity.

In Hungary.

A society has been formed in South Hungary to enable the bride to have her name joined with that of her husband, and it may be noted, in passing, that in Germany and Austria the wife takes the title as well as the name of the man she marries. She is Mrs. Dr. Braun or Mrs. Sanitary Inspector Meyer, Mrs Colonel Schmidt, and so on. The day before a marriage in Hungary there is a grand display of the bride's presents and trousseau, and the more garments, household linen, and beds she has, the prouder she feels. Two matrons and six maids clad in white, each of the latter carrying a crown, escort the bride to church. After the service she goes to her husband's home, where the feast lasts for days with occasional intervals. Each guest may have a dance with and a kiss from the bride, for which payment is made in small coins.

In Switzerland,

as in France, the civil marriage must precede the religious ceremony. A widow or a woman separated from her {112} husband may not marry again till at least ten months have elapsed since the death or deed of separation. At a peasant's wedding there is often a mistress of the ceremonies, who distributes red and blue handkerchiefs among the guests, in return for which she receives money for the bride. The sum thus collected is not given to her till she has been married for forty-eight hours. They marry young, and life is too hard to leave them much leisure for love-making. The Swiss are not an emotional people on the whole, and the head, generally dominates the heart with them. Customs vary according to the locality and the canton in which the marriage takes place.

In Denmark

the same plain gold ring does duty both for betrothal and marriage, the bridegroom changing it from the third finger of the left hand to the third finger of the right at the marriage ceremony.

In France

women of the upper and middle classes often wear no wedding-ring. They seem to regard it as a badge of servitude, and leave it to their humbler sisters. In a Roman Catholic French church the bride is attended by one bridesmaid and a groomsman, who after the service make a collection from the guests and hand it over to the priest. The two perform this act very gracefully. The gentleman turns one hand palm upwards and the lady lets her fingertips rest upon his with her palm downwards, while, as they pass down the aisle together, each holds an alms-bag to the company with the other hand.

At one point in the service both bride and bridegroom are, given lighted candles to hold. Rather risky for the wedding dress! thinks the careful woman. The bride wears a costume similar to that worn in England, but the bridesmaid is in more ordinary afternoon dress, and the same may be said of the guests, who do not assume a distinctively bridal appearance. Sometimes the civil marriage takes place immediately before the religious one, or it may be performed on the preceding day. The Protestant service is of course very simple. Most married men in France wear a wedding-ring.

CHAPTER XX

Runaway Matches--Remarriage of Widows and Widowers--The Children--The Home--Dress--Comparisons.

Runaway Matches.

The old glamour and romance that idealised the runaway match in the days of post-chaises and wayside hostelries have been destroyed by the express train and the telegraph wire. In spite of the change that has come over our social life, the clandestine marriage does still take place; in fact it has been rather boomed in high circles of late; but it might rather be called a "walkaway" than a runaway match. It can all be done in such a quiet, business-like manner that no notice need be drawn to what is going on. The man who urges a young girl into a secret marriage lays himself open to some ugly charges, for parental tyranny is out of date, and that alone provided sufficient excuse for such a grave step.

The man who is mean enough to bind a girl to himself by marriage before he has a home to give her, and then sends her back to her parents as if nothing had happened, is not calculated to make a good husband, unless his offence has the excuse of extreme youth. Let him work his hardest and trust the girl to wait for him. If she will not do that, it is certainly not worth while to commit a dishonourable action for her sake.

The couple who marry and keep the fact a secret because they are afraid of losing some one's money if they tell the truth, would have done better to wait, or to tell each other that love was not good enough without the wherewithal to gild it. In England no one can be forced into a marriage, and all are free to choose whom they like {114} as soon as they are of age; so why stain the start of their wedded life by deception and falsehood? The seeds of distrust and contempt may thus be sown in hearts where there should be mutual love and trust, and then bitter fruits will spring up when once the novelty is over. Given patience, honesty, and fidelity, there need be no secret marriages in this empire.

A private marriage celebrated in the presence of only a few chosen friends is what many may prefer and desire; but considering the inevitable slur contained in the words: "*Why* did they do it?" the woman, at least, would do well to refrain from the sweets of stolen waters.

Second Marriages.

Dr. Johnson pronounced a second marriage to be "The triumph of Hope over Experience." Others who are less epigrammatic affirm that to take a second partner is the highest compliment that can be paid to the departed first. In some cases the real romance of marriage only awakes with the second wooing. It by no means follows that it must be a dull, prosaic, practical transaction.

The Children.

The great question in the remarriage of parents with children under age is the welfare of those children, and the choice of husband or wife, especially the latter, should be largely influenced by this consideration. The step-father is not held in such disfavour as the step-mother, probably because his relations with the young people are not so intimate.

The Widow.

A genial student of womankind says: "A little widow is a dangerous thing! She knows not only her own sex but the other too, and knowledge is power. She is experienced, accessible, and free, and withal fatally fascinating. There is a great charm in loving a woman who is versed in the lore of love, and is practised in all the sleight-of-heart tricks of it." Her courtship is more untrammelled than that of a {115} single woman. Her position is all in her favour. If she is very young, she will probably have a companion, or live with some relative. If she has small children they can afford a very convenient element of propriety when a lover comes to woo.

She does not always have a second engagement ring; she may prefer some other trinket. It is also a matter of taste whether she retain her first wedding-ring in its place or not. If she decides to banish it she should do so before going to be married.

Dress.

Grey is no longer the compulsory shade for a widow's wedding frock. Any light, delicate colour may be worn; but a woman has only one *white* wedding and one bridal veil in her life. The widow is not supposed to make a display over her wedding. An air of somewhat chastened joy is considered more suitable. Instead of bridesmaids she has one lady attendant who should be in her place in church before the bride arrives, and be ready to move to her side when required, to take the gloves and bouquet (which should not be composed of purely white flowers, nor is orange blossom permissible). There may be a second edition of the wedding cake and the presents, but favours and floral tributes are things of the past.

The Home.

If the widow has a nice home of her own she and her husband may decide to live in it; but he will need to exercise tact in taking up his position as master of a household that has hitherto gone on quite well without him. An entire change of servants would probably be advisable if not inevitable. The wife would be careful to give him his full dignity, and not to let it appear that he was to be regarded in the light of a pensioner on her bounty.

The Widower.

A man whose wife dies leaving him with young children, or even one baby, is in a most pathetic position, and the best thing he can do is to find some nice woman to console him and mother the little ones. It is a pity that the two {116} qualifications cannot always go together. It is rather risky for a sister or a niece to regard the home offered her by a widowed brother or uncle as a permanency. Men who are apparently satisfied with existing arrangements have a way of springing surprises upon their devoted womenfolk, and when the new wife appears, the sister or niece who has tided him over the worst part of his life must find a home elsewhere. Of course the man is quite within his rights, but I would warn those who may be living in a fool's paradise.

The widower with a house or estate would, naturally, consult the future mistress of it about any alterations he proposed making before his marriage. On her visits of inspection she would either be chaperoned by her mother or some married relation; but, if more convenient, he would ask a lady friend to come and meet her. If he had a grown-up daughter she would continue to preside over his household till after his marriage. It is not fair for a man to take a second wife without giving any previous intimation to his adult sons and daughters who may still be making their home with him. The installation of a girl step-mother over youths of her own age places them all in rather a difficult position, and has the possible making of a tragedy in it. The widower who marries a spinster may go through all the glories of a smart wedding for a second or third time if he likes, seeing that it is the condition of the bride that decides such matters.

Comparison with the Predecessor.

Those who play the role of No. 2 must make up their minds to be compared, in thought if not in word, involuntarily if not intentionally, with No. 1, and the process need not necessarily be painful. Unless there has been some distressing or tragic element in the first marriage, why should the memory of the dead be banished, except by jealousy or inconstancy? It is not generous of No. 2 to try and sweep away all traces of the predecessor. The man or woman who will lightly abandon all the memories of the partner of youth, is not so calculated to make an ideal companion for middle age as the one who cherishes a tender regard for the dead side by side with an honest love for the living.

CHAPTER XXI

Marrying for Love; for Money; for a Home; for a Housekeeper--Concluding Remarks.

Marrying for Love.

In spite of all that the cynics and pessimists may say, Love should be the Lord of Marriage.

"How sweet the mutual yoke of Man and Wife

When holy fires maintain Love's heavenly life!"

True happiness cannot exist without it, however great the wealth or exalted the position of the married pair may be, while the worst evils of life are lightened and made bearable by its presence. Marrying for love need not mean improvidence. Only an unreasoning passion based on selfishness will plunge the beloved into privation and want. The highest, truest love has its substratum of common sense, self-restraint, and thought for others.

It is very hard to draw the line, for vices and virtues tread somewhat closely on each other's heels. The division between prudence and cowardice is often ill-defined. The love that rushes into poverty that it is not strong enough to endure, has in it an element of the selfishness that makes another sit still in comfort while the path is being made smooth for her soft tread.

There are those who laugh at love, and say that mutual respect and sufficient means are the only two reliable things with which to enter upon matrimony. Both these excellent possessions may, however, be quite compatible with love, in fact the former is bound to be included in the softer passion or it will not wear very well. No one will deny that a marriage founded on mere mutual respect may one day be {118} crowned by true and lasting love; nor yet that pre-matrimonial love may die a speedy or even violent death soon after the lovers are united; but these possibilities do not alter the fact that taking things all round, Love is the best and most precious asset with which to begin married life.

Marrying for Money.

There are many marriages that are casually put under this heading which do not deserve to be. A man's position may be such that it will mean ruin to him if he adds to his expenses by taking a wife without a penny. He honourably refrains from making any advances to girls who are so situated; but that does not prevent his becoming really attached to one whose income will make married life possible for him. The possession of money does not make a woman unlovable for herself, though it may give her an unenviable experience at the hands of the fortune hunter.

The cold, calculating nature that deliberately plans a mercenary marriage is probably satisfied for the time being by the acquisition of the coveted wealth. Little pity will be given when the long-starved human element of the man or woman begins to cry out for something more than money can buy.

There are excuses for some mercenary alliances. The sorely-tried daughter of impecunious parents, whose youth has been clouded by grey, grinding poverty, and who sees the prospects of her brothers and sisters blighted by lack of means to start them in life, is to be pardoned, if not commended, when she marries for money, but she should not deceive the man who gives it to her if she does not love him.

The man with talents and high ambitions may easily be tempted to take the wife whose money will open a field for the realisation of his hopes. He would be more of a man if he fought his way through alone. The curse of it all is that no one marrying for money dares say so. It would be brutal, no doubt; and unless there were some fair equivalent to offer in exchange, probably few such marriages would take place. When the cloak of simulated love is thrown over the real motive, often only to be cast aside as soon as the prize is secured, it is hard not to feel contempt and indignation.

{119} Marriage *with* money is a necessity; marriage *for* money is a mere business affair, a travesty of the sacred institution.

"He that marries for money sells his liberty." It is humiliating enough for a woman, but immeasurably mean in a man.

Marrying for a Home.

The woman with strong domestic instincts, who dreads to face life alone, or has grown weary in the attempt to wage the fight single-handed, often yields to the temptation of marrying one who can give her a home, with only a secondary regard for the man himself. If she duly counts the cost and does not ask too much, the plan may succeed very well; but the entirely domestic woman does not hold the highest place in a man's mind. He may fully value the creature comforts she ensures for him, but she so soon becomes a drudge, and so soon loses touch with the higher side of his nature that he will probably seek sympathy elsewhere, and salve his conscience with the thought that he has given her what she really wanted most.

She must never forget that she has to reckon with the man who has provided her with a home; and she will probably have to repay him in whatever coin he may choose.

Marrying for a Housekeeper.

The man who must keep a home together and maintain appearances grows tired of wrestling with domestic problems, and either dreads the sudden departure of his cook-housekeeper or trembles under her tyrannical sway. He finally takes a lady who cannot give him a month's notice, nor leave his roof by stealth without unpleasant consequences to herself. When he thus primarily marries for a housekeeper who will promote his own comfort, he should be satisfied if she shows the needful domestic efficiency. He sometimes finds that the one who was intended to be little more than a dependant turns out to be his mistress. There are plenty of level-headed women who have done with romance, and who are perfectly willing to take up the position of wife to a man who honestly states that he requires a companion to {120} help his digestion by conversing at meals, to manage his house, entertain his guests, and darn his socks. When such a couple meet together let them show mutual respect for each other's motives, and invest the arrangement with comfort and dignity in the absence of tenderer emotions.

Concluding Remarks.

However short a marriage may fall of the high ideal standpoint, there should never be recrimination in public between man and wife, nor the utterance of taunts as to the avarice, expediency, or cowardice that may have influenced either side in the presence of a third person. Few attain to the highest happiness of which we are capable in this state: few, perhaps, make the most of what they have; yet it is very rare to find a married woman who honestly wishes herself single, and that is a powerful argument in favour of an institution which seems to give the weaker sex her full share of the burden. There is much soul-disquieting discussion nowadays on the relative positions of the sexes. The following lines express that which surely might make marriage a very heaven on earth:--

"This is Woman's need;

To be a beacon when the air is dense,

A bower of peace, a lifelong recompense--

This is the sum of Woman's worldly creed.

And what is Man the while? And what his will?

   And what the furtherance of his worldly hope?

   To turn to Faith, to turn, as to a rope

A drowning sailor; all his blood to spill

For One he loves, to keep her out of ill--

   This is the will of Man, and this his scope."

www.ingramcontent.com/pod-product-compliance
Lightning Source LLC
Chambersburg PA
CBHW081200020426
42333CB00020B/2581